The Complete Book of the
DOG

The Complete Book of the
DOG

Angela Sayer

GALLERY BOOKS
An Imprint of W. H. Smith Publishers Inc.
112 Madison Avenue
New York City 10016

Contents

This book was devised and produced by
Multimedia Books Limited

Editor: Anthony J. Lambert
Consultant Editor: Michael A. Findlay
Production: Arnon Orbach
Design: Behram Kapadia
Picture Research: Pauline Simcock

First published in the United States of America 1989 by
Gallery Books, an imprint of W.H. Smith Publishers Inc.,
112 Madison Avenue, New York, NY 10016.

Reprinted 1991

ISBN 0 8317 1545 6

Origination by D.S. Colour International, London
Jacket originated by Reprocraft Studios (87) Limited
Printed in Italy by Imago Publishing Limited

Half title: The Labrador Retriever
— a perfect water dog and an ideal
house pet. Easily trained,
obedient, kind and docile.

Left: The Great Pyrenean, an
excellent guard.

Title page: The massive Saint
Bernard, descended from the
Alpine Mastiff, is famous for its
rescue work in difficult
snow-covered terrain.

Introduction

For centuries the dog *canis familiaris* and man *homo sapiens* have shared a unique relationship in the natural scheme of things, a relationship which spans the globe and defies all attempts at satisfactory scientific and archeological explanation. Clues to the puzzle are unearthed from time to time and indicate an outline to the dog's evolutionary past which has led scientists to believe that the dog was as important to man's own advancement as fire and the employment of the first stone tools. And though the dog's primary role was probably only utilitarian, strong bonds of affection were quickly forged, as proven by a fairly recent fossil find in Israel. Here, well-preserved remains dating back 12 000 years reveal the skeleton of a man with his hand resting protectively on the head of the dog lying closely by his side.

A pair of German Pointers await their owner's next command. Typically liver in color and with easy-care coats, these dogs are good workers in the field and gentle in the home.

A family of Dingos, the wild dog of Australia, used in the development of such modern breeds as the Kelpie and similar in appearance to feral dogs of other continents.

How dogs evolved

During the geological period of time known as the Eocene, about 40 million years ago, there lived a small weasel-like carnivorous mammal called *Miacis* which was to become the ancestor of bears, civets, cats, hyenas, raccoons, weasels and dogs. During the mid-Oligocene period, *Miacis* died out and another creature, *Cynodictis*, evolved. This in turn evolved to give rise to *Cynodesmus* and *Tomoritus* – forebears of today's canids. In fossil terms, the evolution of today's domestic dog is very recent; the earliest fossil finds date back to about 10 000 BC, which is the point of time when most scientists believe that dog and man began their unique and lasting relationship.

The zoologist Charles Darwin maintained that two species, the Golden Jackal (*Canis aureus*) and the Wolf (*Canis lupus*), are the most likely ancestors of the domestic dog. R.I. Pocock's paper published in 1935 suggested that the genetic information necessary for the production of today's diversity of breeds, types and colors required four types of wolf ancestor. He cited the northen Gray Wolf (*Canis lupus*), the small Desert Wolf (*C.l. arabis*) of Arabia, the pale-footed Asian Wolf (*C.l. palliper*) and the Woolly-coated Wolf or Chinese Wolf (*C.l. laniger*) of Tibet and north India. A great number of mixed matings must have occurred over the centuries, and, with man's eventual hand in selecting for specific characteristics in the dogs he chose for hunting, guarding and fighting, the bases of today's breeds were formed.

Even though dogs now appear in so many shapes, sizes, coat types and colors, all have the same inherent qualities – the legacy of the ancient wolf ancestors.

Above: Though controversy still exists over the close ancestors of today's dogs, this magnificent Timber Wolf shows many features identical to those in several modern breeds.

Below: The Silver-backed Jackal is a cousin of the domestic dog, sharing the same ancestors.

Just as the exact evolutionary process of the dog is shrouded in mystery, so is the exact nature of the relationship between man and dog in the early days of domestication. One theory which seems logical is that early man recognized the dog's superior powers of speed, sight and hearing. Unarmed except for primitive cudgels and stones, man worked hard to hunt and kill his meat. He probably found it beneficial to follow the dog pack, and to drive the animals away from a fresh kill while he helped himself to a substantial portion. The dogs, or perhaps wolves, would stay close by until they could return to their kill, and the close proximity of the two species probably became one of mutual respect and understanding.

Man and wolf had much in common, sharing social systems based on the family, making a degree of organization necessary within each group. Man and wolf had to develop their own hierarchical systems, and, as their relationship became closer, each would recognize this trait in the other. Young wolves or primitive dogs were probably taken into camp by early man, as companions for the children, or even as food. It is possible that the cubs were first taken alive to rear for eating, then formed some bond with the human family, so that they were kept instead as pets and hunting companions.

Above: This family scene in India's Rajasthan shows a Hunting Dog at rest as the bread is baked.

Opposite: The Kalbelias nomads of Rajasthan prepare their famous hunting dogs for the chase, to provide food for the wandering community in which they live.

Above: The Gray Wolf *Canis lupus*, pictured in Alaska, showing traits easily recognizable in today's Husky and the German Shepherd Dog.

Yet another theory of domestication explores the possibility that the dog was first used for guarding rather than for hunting. The dog's superior senses of sight, smell and hearing would have alerted man to all aspects of danger to the camp-site, and the presence of the dogs would have helped to keep predators away.

A final theory suggests that man did not make an active effort to domesticate the dog, but rather a relationship developed naturally, each helping the other on a mutual, and almost accidental basis, the man taking prey from the dog, and the dog scavenging for food scraps, and hunting small rodents living around man's grain stores. The true domestication of the dog would then have been a natural progression. As the dog became more used to all of man's activities, the bolder but less aggressive members of the pack would have approached closer and closer, and in bad weather would perhaps have slunk into the cave for shelter or even moved towards the campfires for warmth. Man's superior intellect would have enabled him to realize that he could dominate the dog by enforcing his will as the leader of the man-dog 'pack'.

The world-wide spread of dogs

No matter how the first bonds were formed between man and dog, it is apparent that they were indeed close companions in Denmark between 8000 and 6000 years ago. Two different types of domesticated dog were discovered in Mesolithic settlements and are generally referred to as the Maglemose Dogs. Other early remains dated at about 4000 BC were discovered in ancient lake settlements in Switzerland. One, known as the Lake Dog, had a very powerful head, with a strong jaw, heavy shoulders and lighter hindquarters. It was probably a hunting dog and able to tackle and hold large prey, and most likely an ancestor of the Spitz group of modern dogs. A second type found in the same deposits is known as the Peat Dog. It has a rounded head with a short muzzle and a jaw of medium strength. It was more likely to have been used for herding than for hunting, and may have been the ancestor of modern pinschers, schnauzers and terriers.

Paleolithic remains found in Russia revealed human and dog bones in close proximity to one another. In this area it seems likely that domestication commenced about 10 000 years ago, and the fossilized dogs were of a now extinct type – *Canis pontiatini* – and very similar to the Lake Dog of Switzerland.

The Ancient Egyptians had several distinct types of dog, obviously selected and developed to perform specific duties. Excavations in Egypt have yielded valuable evidence of early domestication of the dog, and reliefs and artifacts give clear illustrations of their size and conformation. A bas-relief from Thebes, dated 1450 BC, shows two hounds similar to Salukis, pulling down game. Tutankhamun's tomb yielded an ostrich-feather fan decorated with a scene showing the boy king hunting ostriches with a bow and hounds.

Below: These stylized creatures made of finest porcelain in China centuries ago are known as Hell Dogs.

The Ancient Egyptians worshiped dogs and when one died the family would go into a state of mourning, shaving off their eyebrows as a sign of respect, and wailing and beating gongs. Dogs were elaborately preserved and buried with their ornate collars. Some mummified dogs have been found wearing collars bearing their names, such as Ebony and Grabber. The types of dog found include Mastiffs, pointers, Salukis, terriers and a dog similar to today's Pharaoh Hound. There are dogs with both pricked and pendant ears, curled and straight tails, and plain and patterned coats. Mastiffs are shown in battle scenes, while hounds are shown hunting game. A tomb of 2700 BC shows dogs of the Spitz type, while scenes dated at 2000 BC show Greyhounds. From 2000 BC to about 800 BC there is evidence that care was taken in selectively breeding dogs, and there is an increase in the diversity of types of dog.

Dogs were in evidence in the successive civilizations of Sumeria, Babylon and Assyria and were used for retrieving, hunting and digging out game that had gone to ground. On a panel taken from the palace of the Assyrian King Ashurbanipal (669-626 BC) two fierce Mastiffs strain against the leashes by which their handlers control them. On a further panel, the dogs are seen hunting onagers and lions.

The Ancient Greeks bred huge dogs, the Mollossian Mastiffs, and used them for herding and guarding. They also employed special healing dogs whose task was to lick wounds in the temples at Athens. A tablet records this fact thus: 'Thyson of Hermione is blind of both eyes; a temple dog licks the organs and he immediately regains his sight.'

A very well-preserved dog, similar to the Swiss Lake Dog, was excavated in Britain in 1928 at a site called Windmill Hill. This region was inhabited by Neolithic Stone Age man, who came from Europe to colonize southern England around 3000 BC. Two other types of dog were discovered in Dorset in the south of England. One was of the Spitz type, while the other was a powerful Mastiff; they were probably brought to Britain about 500 BC by Phoenician seamen.

As the great trade routes developed and spread, so did the members of the dog family, and each area and culture developed its own types to serve specific functions. Sight hounds were needed for hunting game in open arid lands, and scent hounds were important for hunting game through wooded or undulating country. Large fierce dogs were needed to guard homes, families and flocks, and dogs with natural herding ability were needed as shepherd dogs and drovers.

Above right: A Greek wine jug, dated at BC 540 and discovered on Rhodes, depicts the return from the hunt and shows the successful hunter accompanied by an obviously docile and well-trained dog.

Below right: The Romans' love of dogs is recorded in many ways. Here an ancient bronze lamp is fashioned in the shape of a dog's head, and stands on dog's feet.

Development of Breeds

As civilizations developed, dogs were selectively bred, and the most skilled dogs were used for producing further generations. An appreciation of beauty of form also developed, and dogs were found to have uses other than those of pure utility.

In medieval times, King Alfonso XI of Castile published *Le Libro de la Monteria* which described hunting with hounds in interesting detail, and a vivid complementary account appears in Geoffrey Chaucer's *Boke of the Duchesse* written twenty years later in 1370. In 1387, Gaston Phoebus wrote *Livre de Chasse* which was translated into English twenty years later by Edward, second Duke of York, who also added information about English dogs and hunting procedures, publishing the resulting work under the title *The Master of Game*. The book makes mention of a variety of hounds each used for a different purpose. There were the Couchers, forebears of today's spaniels and setters; Bloodhounds, possessed of superior scenting powers and forebears of the modern scent hounds; and Kennets and Harriers, used for driving deer into the path of the bowmen, which may be the ancestors of some of today's terriers. It is clear from medieval portraits that tiny lapdogs were in favor and they are depicted asleep on cushions, or on the laps of their doting masters and mistresses.

In 1479 Dame Juliana Bernes' *The Boke of St Albans* was published, and described the canine 'breeds' of the day in interesting detail. Although all the dogs are referred to as hounds, it is clear that not all were used for hunting: 'fyrste there is a Greyhoun, a Bastard, a Mengrell, a Mastif, a Lemor, a Spanyel; Raches and Kenettys; Teroures; Butchers Houndes, Dunghyll dogges; Trydeltaylles and Pryckeryd currys; and small ladyes popees that bere aweay the flees...'

In the sixteenth and seventeenth centuries everyone of note competed for the privilege of owning and displaying the finest dogs that money could buy. Pride of ownership embraced the fiercest of guard dogs, the fleetest of hounds, terriers which became champions of the rat pit, bulldogs which would bait bears as well as bulls, and the tiniest of toy lapdogs.

In 1604 it is recorded that twenty specially selected Mastiff bitches were kept for breeding bear-baiting dogs at the court of England's James I. Large Mastiff types were used in the bear-pit, while a smaller stockier dog was necessary for bull-baiting. The values of successful dogs soared, and the science of dog-breeding began.

Eventually, on May 30, 1850, the first recorded dog show took place in London and was described as a 'Great Exhibition of the Pugs of All Nations'; it was a small, social affair in aid of charity. The following year, however, there was 'A Fancy Dog Show' held in the bar parlor of a public house in London's Denmark Street. The exhibitors were formed into the first recorded association of dog fanciers, and the exhibits included King Charles and Blenheim Spaniels, Italian Greyhounds and Isle of Skye Terriers. Rival dog clubs quickly formed, and one set up a series of shows, each advertised as a 'Grand Show of Spaniels, Terriers, Small Dogs, etc.' Dogs were offered for sale, male dogs were available for stud purposes at these shows and, before long, show notices were advertising exciting news of freshly imported breeds.

In 1859, the first officially recognized dog show was staged in Newcastle-upon-Tyne in England, and it set the standard for shows throughout Europe. The English Kennel Club was formed in 1873, and the American Kennel Club was established on September 17, 1884. A century has followed of growing interest in dogs, their breeding and showing.

Left: A tapestry from Tournai, Belgium, made about 1430 AD shows typical hounds of the time hunting the bear, and holding a wild boar at bay.

Below: An early hunting scene shows how using hounds to procure food evolved into sporting events. These hounds of uniform type and coloration show the care taken with their breeding. *The Hunt* by Paolo Uccello

Development of breeds

The Romans valued their dogs, using large animals in battle and as guards. They used dogs as sacrificial offerings, too, in an attempt to protect precious crops from the searing summer sun, during the dog-days of August, when Sirius, the Dog Star, was in its ascent.

When the Romans invaded Britain in 54 BC they were astonished to find large ferocious dogs fighting alongside the Britons. This fact was reported back to Rome, and eventually a Procurator, Cynegli, was appointed to travel to Britain in order to find and procure dogs to be pitted against bulls, bears, lions and tigers in the circus at Rome. The Romans called the muscular British fighting dog *Canis pugnax*, and these dogs fought and beat every fighting dog pitted against them, even the massive Mollossian Mastiffs. Regular exports to Rome were made from England, Scotland and, later, Ireland; later still, English and Welsh scent hounds were exported for hunting.

After the eclipse of the Roman Empire there are large gaps in the written history of the domestic dog; nevertheless we know that dogs were selectively bred for carrying out their special duties, and that there was great pride taken in the prowess of certain dogs.

About 1000 years ago, in the golden age of Hywell Dda, this King of Wales set down specific laws relating to dogs: 'There are three higher kinds of dog – the dog which hunts by sight, the greyhound and the spaniel. There are three kinds of dog which hunt by scent – the bloodhound, the covert hound and the harrier. There are three kinds of curs – the mastiff, the shepherd dog and the housedog.'

Strict fines were imposed for killing a dog. Each fine was known as the bloodprice and was proportional to the rank of the dog's master. One of the king's covert hounds was valued at one pound; a similar dog owned by a nobleman would be worth only half that price; one owned by a peasant would be worth a groat, a sixtieth part of a pound. The bloodprice of a shepherd dog was determined by its abilities, and a valuable dog of this type would be one capable of leading out the cattle at dawn, driving them home at night and then standing night watch.

In other parts of Europe at the same time, a shepherding dog was highly valued if it was capable of attacking a wolf, taking a young lamb from the jaws of a wolf, and alerting neighboring farms.

Above left: Taken from a frieze of the ruined palace of Ashurbanipal's palace at Nineveh, this fragment shows Ancient Assyrian warriors exercising their great war dogs in the royal park.

Below left: Three thousand years old, Egyptian gazehounds search for game from the frescoes of the Temple of Kom Ombo in the Nile Valley, Egypt.

Right: Taken from the Bayeaux Tapestry, recording the events of 1066 AD, this portion shows England's King Harold mounted on a fine stallion, with his falcon on his wrist and accompanied by hounds and terriers.

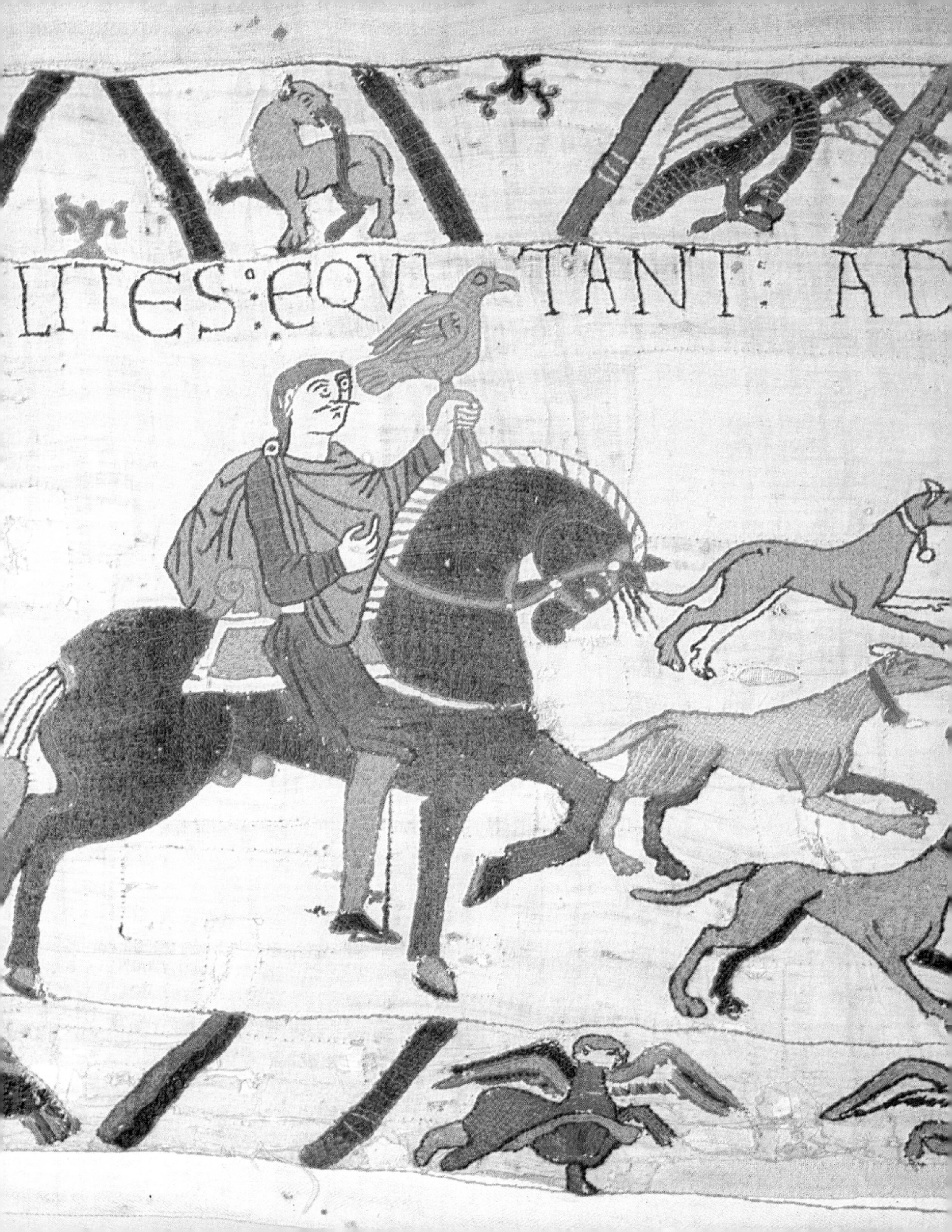
LITES:EQVI TANT: AD

Anatomy and lifestyle

It is important for the dog owner to understand as much as possible about his dog, and a knowledge of the way in which its body is constructed and functions enables better standards of feeding, care and general husbandry.

An insight into the dog's natural patterns of behavior is an aid to understanding and training, while a study of the reproductive systems of the dog and bitch will help the novice to decide whether or not to breed a litter of puppies.

The English Cocker Spaniel can make a perfect pet.

19

The skeleton

The skeleton of the dog is referred to in two parts: the axial skeleton and the appendicular skeleton. The axial skeleton includes the skull, which varies considerably from breed to breed while retaining the same essential characteristics. The spinal column is also part of the axial structure, and starts with the seven cervical vertebrae which form the neck. At the head end, the first vertebra, known as the Atlas, permits the head to move up and down, while the second vertebra, the Axis, enables the head and the Atlas to rotate. The remaining cervical vertebrae allow the dog sufficient flexibility to turn the neck to look directly behind, without moving the body. Below the neck, thirteen thoracic vertebrae protect the spinal cord and support the thirteen pairs of ribs which form a flexible ribcage to protect the heart and lungs. From the end of the ribcage, seven lumbar vertebrae support the abdomen and lead to the sacrum, which usually consists of three fused vertebrae, followed by a series of caudal vertebrae which form the tail. However, this feature varies greatly from breed to breed.

The appendicular skeleton consists of the forelimbs and hindlimbs. The forelimb has a strong flattened shoulder blade or scapula, attached by strong muscles to the skeleton. At its lower end it is connected via a highly flexible joint to the humerus. The lower end of

This Lurcher ably illustrates the structure of a typical dog.

the humerus is attached to paired bones, the radius and the ulna. Moving further down, the radius and ulna meet the carpal joint. This is equivalent to the human wrist and is made up of several small bones, arranged in two rows, and forming a joint with the foot. The carpal joint moves mainly by flexion and extension, but is also capable of some rotation. The dog's foot has a series of five metacarpal bones, side by side, and each metacarpal has a corresponding digit consisting of three phalanges, the third of which is covered by a claw. The inside digit is the smallest, and may be absent in some dogs. When present it is known as the dew-claw.

The hind limb is attached to the pelvic girdle, which is formed of three paired bones fused into a ring-shaped structure, and attached to the axial skeleton at the sacrum. On either side of the girdle is a depression called the acetabulum which provides a socket for the head of the femur or thigh bone. The lower end of the femur articulates with the partly fused tibia and fibula. This joint, known as the stifle joint, is protected by the patella or kneecap. At the lower end of the tibia the hock joint, or tarsal, is equivalent to the carpus in the forelimb, and the hindfoot has the same basic structure as the forefoot, though the dew-claw is rarer in the hindlimbs.

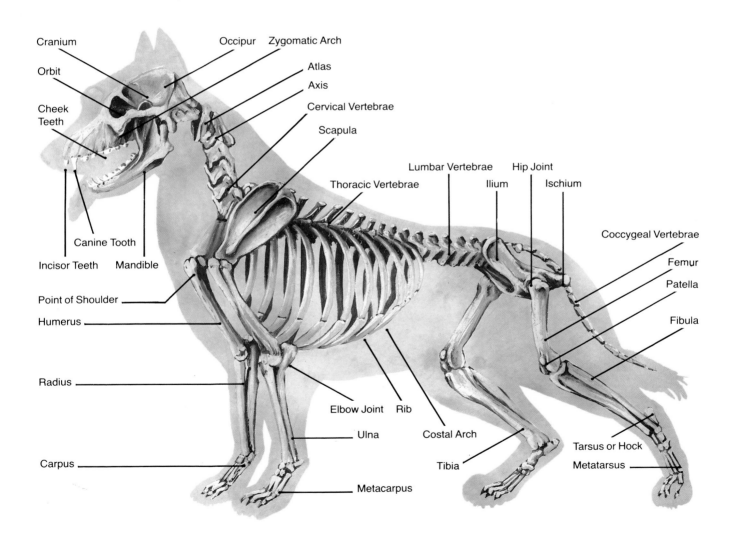

Muscles and nerves

The dog's skeleton is covered by layers of muscles which precisely control the animal's movement. Muscles act in pairs or groups, in which some contract to bend a joint, while others contract to straighten a joint. As a muscle contracts it swells. Muscles are richly supplied with blood vessels, as well as with nerves. Different muscles have different functions, depending on whether, for instance, they are part of the system which controls the limbs or whether they form the muscular walls of the heart, chest or abdomen. All act in the same basic manner, however, by contracting and relaxing. The heart beats because of the involuntary regular contraction and relaxation of its muscles. In the same way the chest muscles constantly expand and contract the ribcage, causing an intake of air into the lungs, and pushing used air out again.

The muscles which enable the dog to move its limbs are called locomotor muscles, and are attached to the various bones of the appendicular skeleton. As the individual muscles contract they draw together the bones to which they are attached, and as they relax they allow the bones to move apart. This enables the joint to flex or extend and thus the limbs to move.

Muscular control is directed from the brain via nerve cells. Instructions are transmitted along the spinal cord and then to the nerves in the muscles. The nerves also carry messages back to the brain, reporting pain or sensations such as warmth, cold and so on.

The dog's structure allows a degree of upward leaping movement as well as normal running and loping.

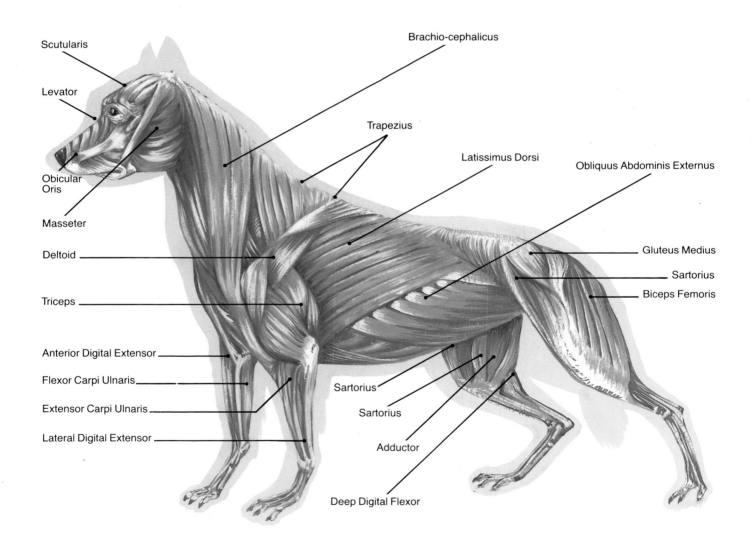

Scutularis

Levator

Obicular Oris

Masseter

Deltoid

Triceps

Anterior Digital Extensor

Flexor Carpi Ulnaris

Extensor Carpi Ulnaris

Lateral Digital Extensor

Brachio-cephalicus

Trapezius

Latissimus Dorsi

Obliquus Abdominis Externus

Gluteus Medius

Sartorius

Biceps Femoris

Sartorius

Sartorius

Adductor

Deep Digital Flexor

The alimentary canal

The alimentary canal is, in effect, a tube of varying size which begins at the mouth of the dog and ends at the anus. In the mouth the dog's tongue is used for lapping fluids and licking small particles of solid food. The tongue is also used to soften hard food by mixing it with the enzymes contained within the saliva. The dog's teeth are also very important in the digestive process. In the wild some of the teeth are used to kill the prey, and others are used to remove meat from the carcass and slice it into easily swallowed pieces. Despite the great diversity of form of dogs' jaws, all have the same number and distribution of teeth. The side of each jaw should have three incisors, one canine, and four premolars in both upper and lower sets, and there are two molars in each side of the upper jaw and three in the lower set. Three pairs of salivary glands produce the saliva that is emptied into the mouth prior to and during feeding, to soften the food before it is swallowed.

From the mouth the food passes down the esophagus and into the stomach, where enzymes and acids reduce the food for passage through the pylorus, a ring-shaped muscle at the lower end of the stomach. Food passes through the pylorus into the small intestine from where nutrients are extracted which pass into the bloodstream; then the remains of the material pass into the large intestine. In the large intestine fluid is extracted, and the bulk of the remaining material passes into the rectum, and out through the anus as feces.

Other organs play vital roles in the digestive process. Near the small intestine is the pancreas, a gland which produces insulin to control the consistency of the feces. The liver's main function is to aid the digestion of food in the stomach and the small intestine. It also produces a substance called bile to assist in the breakdown of fats; excess bile is stored in the gall bladder. The liver also stores some soluble food substances.

The urinary tract consists chiefly of the paired kidneys, which receive and filter the blood that has passed around the body. The waste matter filtered out forms urine and is passed down the ureters to the bladder to be temporarily stored. At intervals the sphincter muscle at the lower end of the bladder is relaxed and the urine is allowed to flow out. In the male dog it passes through the penis to the outside, while in the female the urethra empties into the vagina and the urine is passed out of the body via the vulva.

The skin and lungs also expel waste products from the dog's body; the skin by direct transmission into the atmosphere and the lungs by the expulsion of waste gases via the trachea into the atmosphere.

The dog's alimentary canal begins in the mouth, where its efficient teeth and tongue start the processes of digestion.

Respiration-circulation

Respiration consists of drawing oxygen in the air into the body and then expelling waste gases. Air is taken in via the nostrils and passes through the pharynx at the back of the throat, then through the larynx to the trachea or windpipe. The trachea passes down the neck and into the chest, where it divides into two bronchi, one connected to each lung. Each bronchus splits into a series of small air passages called bronchioles, forming a system through which air passes into the functioning cells of the lungs and from where oxygen is diffused into the dog's bloodstream. The waste gases carbon dioxide and nitrogen are exhaled through the nostrils into the atmosphere.

The dog's nostrils are used for scenting as well as breathing. Air is drawn in through the nasal cavities and over the specialized cells that register the sensation of smell. Most dogs have exceptional powers of smell, having a greater length of nasal passage than most other animals, and a correspondingly larger region of the brain for assimilating the information brought by the nasal apparatus. They also have scroll-shaped bones within the nose. These structures, known as turbinates, greatly increase the number of scent cells.

The circulatory system consists of the heart and the blood vessels that transport blood between the heart and the organs and tissues. Arteries lead away from the heart carrying blood rich with oxygen from the lungs. The arteries become narrower the further they are from the heart. Smaller arteries are called arterioles, and the tiniest are called capillaries. Blood is pumped through the arterial network by the beating of the heart, and it is the pumping action which produces the dog's pulse.

Arterial blood is bright red while venous blood is darker and is returned to the lungs, where it is reoxygenated, and the heart via venules and veins. Veins, and the smaller venules, are generally wider than arteries, but have thinner walls and do not pulsate. Blood carries nourishment to every cell in the dog's body, and removes waste products. Every tissue, bone, muscle and organ has its own arterioles bringing in oxygenated blood and corresponding venules carrying away the waste-filled blood. The spleen, lying near the stomach, filters out spent blood cells and helps to manufacture new ones.

When swimming the dog's respiration rate steadies and it carries its nose clear of the water, propeling itself forward with paddling movements of the four limbs.

Larynx

Lungs   Esophagus

Jugular Vein

Trachea

Diaphragm

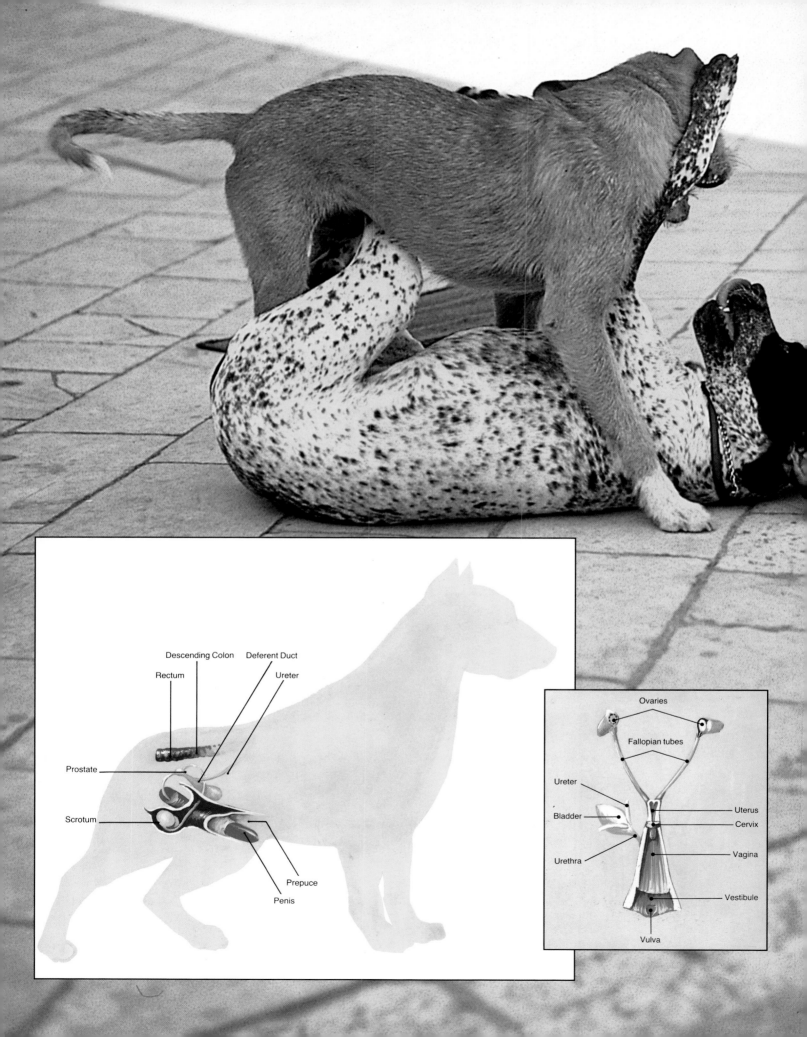

Descending Colon   Deferent Duct

Rectum   Ureter

Prostate

Scrotum

Prepuce

Penis

Ovaries

Fallopian tubes

Ureter   Uterus

Bladder   Cervix

Vagina

Urethra

Vestibule

Vulva

The reproductive organs follow the typical mammalian pattern. The penis lies outside the body and in a bony structure enveloping the urethra at the internal end. The urethra is a narrow channel for the passage of both urine and seminal fluid. A pair of testes lie in a pouch of skin, known as the scrotal sac, between the dog's thighs. The testes produce male hormones and the spermatozoa necessary for reproduction, and this is stored in layers of epididymis on the upper surface of each testicle. During mating spermatozoa and hormones pass from the epididymis along the *ducta deferens*, a tube leading to the urethra, and here they meet seminal fluid manufactured by the prostate gland. The seminal fluid carries the spermatozoa through the penis where it is ejaculated.

In the bitch, the only visible portion of the reproductive system is the vulva, which forms the end of the genital canal. The vulva leads to the vagina, into which the male's penis is inserted during mating, and through which the puppy emerges at birth. At the top of the vagina is a valve-like structure called the cervix, which separates the vagina from the uterus. The uterus has two branches or 'horns', each leading to a Fallopian tube and ovary. The ovary produces hormones and eggs.

Most female dogs come into breeding season twice a year, after reaching puberty at any time between six and fourteen months of age. The season or 'heat' lasts about twenty-one days and follows a set pattern. The first sign of heat in the bitch is a marked enlargement of the vulva, soon followed by the discharge of an opaque liquid, which gradually changes to a blood-stained fluid. This red discharge occurs when the walls of the uterus undergo changes in preparation for receiving fertilized eggs. The red discharge lasts for about ten days during which time the bitch attracts male dogs, but is unwilling to mate. During exercise, the bitch passes frequent drops of urine, and these appear to attract the attentions of male dogs from a wide area. From the tenth day, a light, straw-colored discharge replaces the bloodstained one, and the bitch is in mating condition and will accept the attentions of the male. The bitch will normally mate from the tenth to the fourteenth day after the onset of heat, but may accept a male until the twenty-first day if conception has not taken place. The vulva regains its normal size about three weeks after the onset of estrus.

During mating seminal fluid is released via the penis into the vagina, and the spermatozoa propel themselves towards the cervix. This opens, allowing access to the uterus and Fallopian tubes where the eggs are stored. Once the eggs are fertilized, they travel into the uterus and implant themselves in its richly lined walls. Successfully implanted, the fertilized eggs form embryos which develop into puppies, ready for birth after sixty-three days.

At the beginning of estrus, the bitch's odor may attract the attention of the male dog, but she will be unwilling to mate and will repel his advances.

Genetics

Genetics is the study of inherited characteristics, and explains how features of the parents are transmitted to their offspring. Inherited traits may be both physical and mental, and in some cases may be modified by environmental factors such as daylight, diet, solitude or stimulation.

Genes are units of hereditary material present in the reproductive cells, and are carried in thread-like bodies called chromosomes. Each species has a specific number of chromosomes which always occur in pairs, and in the dog the number of chromosome pairs in each cell is 39. Each individual has two genes of each kind in its makeup; one of these is derived from its father, and the other from its mother. Each gene may be either dominant or recessive in character to the other member of its pair, and it is the balance of the genes that gives each individual its own unique appearance. It is the careful application of a knowledge of genetics that enables breeders to juggle with genes in order to fix certain characteristics and colors in their dogs, and also to eliminate unwanted traits.

In dealing with certain inherited defects in the dog, the science of genetics has helped to reduce the incidence of affected animals. The two best known examples which have received the support of governing and veterinary bodies are schemes to control hip dysplasia and progressive retinal atrophy.

To the breeder interested in one basic breed, the science of genetics is useful as a tool in eliminating unwanted features, and in introducing or fixing desired features. Even before genetics was widely understood, breeders were unknowingly using the science by merely choosing their breeding dogs and bitches from animals exhibiting the characters that were most desired, and mating them together. Offspring with unwanted traits were discarded, and further generations were bred from the puppies that most nearly conformed to the ideal. In this way, man imposed unnatural selection on his dogs and produced the nucleus stock of the many diverse breeds of today.

In applying the science of genetics to breeding, it is necessary to determine which among the characters important to the breed in question are dominant and which are recessive. A dog which carries two genes for a certain characteristic is said to be homozygous for that character. A dog whose appearance suggests that it is of a certain character, but which is known to 'carry' the gene for its alternative recessive character, is said to be heterozygous for the character.

An example of how the genes work can be seen from the simplified charts which show how the dominant and recessive characteristics work in relation to one another. The dominant dog could be black, and the recessive dog could be blue; any other pair of genes could be chosen, however, and the same example charts will produce corresponding results.

Note: It is important to realize that the charts below only represent the expected proportions of offspring: the inheritance of the dominant or recessive gene is pure chance in each fusing and therefore the proportions will not hold true for every group of four puppies born.

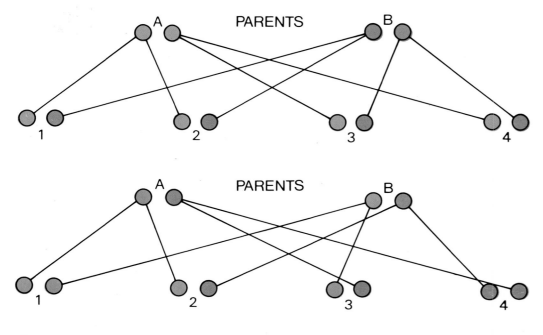

PARENTS

PARENTS

⬤ Dominant gene
◯ Recessive gene

Upper example: The puppies all look like parent A but 'carry' the character of parent B.

Lower example: Puppies 1, 2 and 3 all look like the parents and grandparent A; 1 is exactly like grandparent A, and does not 'carry' recessive character; 2 and 3 are like the parents, and 'carry' the recessive character; 4 is like grandparent B, and homozygous for the recessive character.

Right: The appearance of every dog is determined by its genetic makeup. Half of its genes are inherited from its father, and half from its mother, and the manipulation of dogs' genes by selected matings over the centuries led to the development of today's breeds.

Social behavior

The dog is essentially a pack animal, and that is probably why it has become such a willing part of man's family – which, after all, is only another type of pack. Dogs enjoy being in the company of others, when they quickly revert to pack behavior, doing the same things at the same time, eating together, resting together and supporting one another when threatened. Some individuals are dominant towards others, and an order of rank is formed within the dog group. In the family, where the dog becomes part of the human pack, it has to find its position in the order of rank, and once this is accepted by all parties, the dog will be content.

The highly social dog needs to learn how to live with other dogs and pets, as well as within the family group. Research has shown that there is a brief period in puppyhood when the young dog learns to accept socialization. Because of this it has been accepted that the best time to remove a puppy from its mother and siblings is between six and eight weeks of age. If this is done, the young dog will accept other dogs in a friendly way, and will socialize readily with humans.

At this age it should be introduced to other animals with which it will live, such as cats and farm livestock.

If a puppy is removed from the bitch at too early an age, and reared in a home without other dogs, it may become too humanized and be unable to relate to other dogs in later life. Conversely, puppies left in semi-isolation with the bitch and litter mates until thirteen weeks of age, and with very little human contact, will never adjust well to life with a human family.

The dog's sense of smell is probably a hundred times more sensitive than that of a human being, and its nose, as a scenting organ, is important for all aspects of daily life. A dog out for a walk uses its nose all the time, testing and exploring every scent that comes its way. It is this sense that enables a lost dog to find its way home, to recognize its master, no matter how he or she is disguised, and to track and hunt. The dog's hearing is also far superior to that of man and more sensitive in high frequency sounds. Dogs often get ready to greet a member of the family long before anyone else hears the car or the approaching footsteps.

Except for the long-sighted ability of some of the sight hounds, dogs generally have eyesight on a par with that of man. The dog sees moving objects well, but during daylight poor visual acuity prevents the dog from distinguishing perfectly still or hidden objects or prey except by scenting. In dim light, however, the dog's vision is better than man's, and the dog has better peripheral vision, giving a larger visual field. Dogs probably see some color, but do not see the same spectrum as the human.

Dogs are able to communicate very well, not only with one another but also with other species and with their owners. Dogs use every sort of communication method, natural and contrived. They make sounds of various sorts, use body language and give off chemical signals. The dog uses its eyes to stare out another dog, and the submissive dog will look away. A human can stare at his dog, and it will soon look away and may roll over in a submissive posture. An aggressive dog, or one protecting property, will respond dramatically to a stare and might attack. The ears are indicators of expression, too; erect ears show alertness, and ears held back against the head indicate feelings of submission or fear.

The tail also indicates emotions: a wagging tail indicates excitement; a high tail means alertness; a low tail shows submission; and a tail tucked between the legs shows fear.

When dogs first meet one another they usually smell each other nose to nose, then smell each other's genital regions. Body language is important, too, and the stiffness of the legs, the attitude of the head and ears, and the position of the tail all communicate one dog's feelings and responses to the other.

The male dog covers all manner of objects with small drops of urine in order to mark his territory. In particular he will mark any object previously marked by other dogs. To leave a more definitive mark, the dog defecates, then, using its hind feet, scratches vigorously at the ground, releasing pheromones, which are special chemical scent markers, from glands between the toes. The feces themselves are used as scent markers, and receive the dog's individual odor from secretions produced by the anal glands during the act of defecation. In bitches, the urine undergoes changes during estrus, and the scent from this attracts male dogs from a wide area.

Dogs also communicate through making and hearing sounds which include barking, howling and whining. Barking is very variable and owners come to recognize the tones and nuances which have different meanings, just as the dog soon comes to recognize the intonations in its master's voice.

Above: Within the human family group the dog must establish its own identity and place in the dominance scale. This Border Terrier probably considers itself just beneath the child in the family order of hierarchy.

Left: In the Husky team dogs confront one another until an order of dominance is established and a true leader emerges.

Right: A Pointer puppy makes submissive gestures towards the older dog. This action is similar to the food-soliciting behavior seen in wild dog packs.

Aggression and play

Puppies learn by play, gaining skills for later use in fighting, hunting, chasing and mating. The bitch plays with her puppies, puppies play with one another and, later, the young dog plays with its new master, forming a life-long bond. Adult dogs often indulge in play, too, and very occasionally this gets out of hand and turns into a fight, showing how close is the relationship between aggression and play.

The basic form of aggression in the dog may be termed predatory aggression, where the dog becomes excited and chases prey, or another dog. Territorial aggression is generally directed against humans, particularly those who appear threatening, or in uniform like the mailman. It is sometimes directed against other dogs, too, particularly those which threaten the dog's own position in a hierarchy. Male dogs are prone to picking fights with other male dogs, and bitches sometimes pick fights with one another,

but it is very rare for a male and female to fight. A bitch with puppies is liable to attack any dog which threatens her litter, and may be aggressive to humans, and to other intrusive pets.

Aggression induced by fear is the cause of most dog bites in humans and in other dogs. The frightened dog misinterprets the gestures of others and bites in self-defense. Pain-induced aggression has a similar cause and effect, and the dog snaps at the vet who is giving an injection, or its owner who is removing a thorn, and so on.

Early play and socialization is vital in reducing the likelihood of aggression in the dog. During play, permanent bonds are formed and the dog learns trust and confidence. A happy, well-balanced dog will rarely show aggression, but will still retain sufficient natural defensive instincts to make an efficient watchdog.

Above: Play and socialization play an important role in the life of the young dog, and dogs expected to live happily with animals of other species must be introduced to them at an early age.

Right: To reduce the likelihood of an aggressive disposition, it is important for puppies to play, like these Dalmatians.

Sex and mating

Having reached the age of puberty, the male dog is always ready for mating, and does not have periods of heat. Only when a bitch releases special pheromones does the dog make any sexual advances towards her, however. Before the act of mating, dogs generally indulge in courtship. This takes the form of mutual smelling and play fighting, then the bitch assumes the typical mating posture standing straight and firm, and with the tail held to one side. During mating the dog mounts the bitch, clasping her about the ribcage with his forelegs, and brings his penis close to the vulva to enable penetration to occur.

The genitals of the dog family are unique in having a structure called the *bulbus glandis* in the penis. After ejaculation, this swells like a balloon within the vagina of the bitch, locking the two animals together in a position known as the 'tie'. Though locked together in this way, the dog may dismount from the bitch by lifting a leg over her rump, and the two animals will remain joined, but now back to back, for about twenty minutes. Eventually the swelling in the *bulbus glandis* subsides and the dogs draw apart. Then the male licks his penis until it returns to its sheath.

Breeders usually allow the dog and bitch to mate two or three times to guarantee fertilization. Often the act of mating is highly supervised, and assisted by two or three helpers. Most veterinary experts prefer the natural method, where the bitch is allowed to live with the dog for three or four days, and matings take place when both animals are ready.

Above: Play behavior may include mock fights as shown by these two Indian dogs gamboling and pretending to grasp one another by the throat.

Below: Dogs recognize one another by scent and when two dogs meet, it is usual for them to examine and test the body scent of one another and to sniff at recent excretions.

The pregnant bitch shows little sign of her condition for the first month after mating. She neither requires nor seeks any extra food or attention, and her behavior follows its normal patterns. Around the fifth week, however, she appears a little stockier around the body, just behind the ribs, and her breasts appear a little swollen, or more pronounced. She might be a little erratic with her diet, sometimes demanding more food, sometimes leaving her meal. During the sixth week of her pregnancy the bitch's diet should be modified by adding extra rations of high-protein ingredients, and splitting the total food into two or three meals during the day, rather than feeding a snack and a main meal.

During the last three weeks of the gestation period the embryo puppies grow at a dramatic rate, and this has an equally dramatic effect on the outline of the bitch. As the birth date approaches, the bitch may go off her food, and she must be provided with a comfortable and acceptable place in which to give birth to her litter.

Below: A Basset Hound bitch approaching the end of her pregnancy.

The process of birth in the bitch is generally referred to as whelping, and takes place approximately 63 days after mating. When the birth is imminent, the bitch becomes restless, refuses food, and may exhibit very heavy panting. This stage is the most distressing for both the bitch and her owner, and places them under considerable stress. The bitch should be encouraged to go into her whelping box, well away from the hustle of family life, where she can be calm and quiet. The panting stage can last for twelve hours, or even longer, then the natural hormonal action causes the first puppy's placenta to separate from the wall of the uterus and the expelling pains begin. The puppy, in its sac and surrounded by another sac filled with fluid, passes through the cervix and vagina and out into the world. One or two expelling pains force the fluid bag to the vulva, and another contraction pushes the puppy through. Puppies born head first pass out quite smoothly; with those born tail first sometimes a little extra help is needed in delivering the head.

The bitch normally licks the fetal sac from the puppy's head as soon as it is born, enabling it to take its first breath of air. The bitch then licks away the sac and swallows all the membranes. The placenta, still attached to the puppy by the umbilical cord, may be delivered along with the puppy, or will be expelled a few minutes later. The bitch severs the cord and swallows the placenta. In the wild, eating the nourishing placenta from each puppy ensures her of a valuable meal when she would be unable to hunt, but in a domestic situation it is better for the bitch to eat only three or four placentas, otherwise she may get diarrhea. The bitch licks the puppy dry and encourages it to nurse. Subsequent puppies are born in the same way, and the bitch usually deals with each in turn, and cleans the bedding and her own body between labor pains.

At birth puppies quickly become chilled and suffer cold damage from which they may not fully recover. It is not always practical to hang heat lamps over the whelping box as the bitch may be overheated, so it is important to keep an eye on the temperature of the newborn puppies. If they become cold and start to cry, place a warm hot water bottle near them. Polyester fur bedding is ideal for whelping as it allows liquids to pass through while the surface remains dry and warm.

Some bitches whelp easily and the puppies arrive at intervals of about twenty minutes or so, allowing time for each to be cleaned and dried before the next arrival. Other bitches take longer to produce their puppies, with intervals of an hour or even two hours between. A very long labor can tire a bitch and she may need veterinary attention. She should never be allowed to strain without making any progress or she will become exhausted, and may lose some of her puppies. Occasionally, when a puppy is malpresented or too large to pass naturally into the world, it may need to be delivered by Cesarian section.

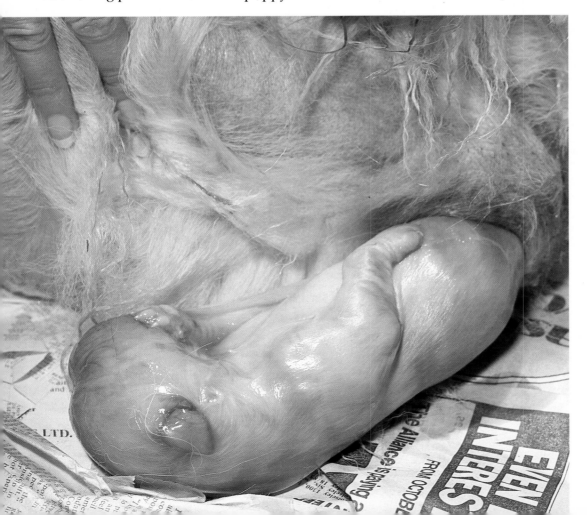

Left: A newborn puppy is delivered completely encased within a fetal sac, surrounded by fluid. Here the head and body are free while the hind legs remain within the bitch's body.

Right: Shortly after birth, having been cleaned and stimulated by the mother's rough tongue, the tiny blind puppy finds its way to a nipple and begins to take the bitch's nourishing milk.

Soon after birth the puppy instinctively moves to the warm underbelly of the bitch and nuzzles around to find a teat. The bitch's mammary glands secrete colostrum, a watery milk which contains important antibodies to protect the puppies during the first weeks of life. During the first weeks of lactation the bitch has a red discharge from the vulva, and, if this becomes offensive or if she neglects to clean it away, veterinary attention should be sought in case she has a retained placenta, or some other trouble in the uterus.

The bitch requires extra food and plenty of fresh water while she is lactating; otherwise, the litter requires little attention during the first few weeks. The puppies are born blind and deaf but with a keen sense of smell. Eyes open at ten days and hearing sharpens at around three weeks, when the puppies are moving unsteadily around the box. While the puppies are feeding on her own milk the bitch washes them and stimulates them to urinate and defecate by licking the genital regions. She swallows all their excretions, keeping the whelping box clean and odor-free. The bitch's rich milk puts rapid growth and weight on the puppies, but they will accept solid feeds from a fairly early age. Some breeders start supplementary feeding of milk and baby cereal in order to relieve pressure on the mother; others prefer to wait until the puppies are old enough to accept finely ground meat.

The puppies' teeth come through at two to three weeks, and the second set of teeth at four to six months.

Even when the puppies are weaned, the bitch will enjoy playing with them and teaching them skills. Some breeders take the bitch away from the litter as soon as possible so that the mother may regain her original shape and strength, but this is sad, and puppies left with the mother seem to grow better and have steadier temperaments than those weaned and removed early.

Puppies show a rapid rate of growth if correctly fed, and given four meals a day after weaning. The best method is to feed to the individual's appetite and remove any uneaten food after ten to fifteen minutes. Never feed between meals, and always have fresh drinking water available. A puppy of a medium-sized breed (about 30 lb when adult) will treble its weight between two and four months of age; in the following two months it will increase by 40 to 50 percent, and by the age of ten months it will have achieved 90 percent of its adult weight. The very large breeds develop more slowly.

To weigh your puppy, first weigh yourself on your bathroom scales, then weigh yourself again with the puppy in your arms. Deduct the first reading from the second to give the weight of the puppy. Small breeds

may be placed on the kitchen scales, or placed in a bag and weighed with a spring balance. Any distinct check in the steady weight gain should be corrected by increasing the rations.

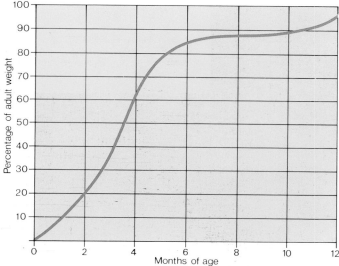

Right: The bitch cleans away all traces of urine and feces passed by her puppies until they start eating solid foods.

Left: A magnificent Rhodesian Ridgeback bitch protects her sturdy puppies as they enjoy their first day out on the lawn.

Right: A healthy, alert and obviously well-reared young puppy, ready to go to its new owners.

Immunization program

Vaccine	Age of vaccination
Canine distemper virus	First: 6-8 weeks Second: 10-12 weeks Third: 14-16 weeks Revaccinate: annually or First: 6-8 weeks Second: 12-16 weeks Revaccinate: annually
Measles virus	6-8 weeks DO NOT vaccinate pregnant bitches or adult dogs
Infectious canine hepatitis virus (Canine adenovirus 1: CAV 1)	Usually given in combination with canine distemper vaccine *Vaccination with CAV 1 vaccine protects against CAV 2 disease
Infectious canine laryngo-tracheitis virus (Canine adenovirus 2: CAV 2)	Usually given in combination with canine distemper vaccine *Vaccination with CAV 2 vaccine protects against CAV 1 disease
Canine parainfluenza virus	**Parenteral vaccine:** usually given in combination with canine distemper and CAV vaccine. If given alone, two doses at 4-week intervals; revaccinate annually **Intranasal vaccine:** combined with a modified-live *Bordetella bronchiseptica* vaccine. One dose only; puppies may be vaccinated from 2-3 weeks of age; revaccinate annually
Bordetella bronchiseptica	**Parenteral vaccine:** Killed *Bordetella* vaccine can be given to pups at 3-5 weeks of age; usually given in combination with canine distemper vaccine; revaccinate annually **Intranasal vaccine:** modified-live *Bordetella* vaccine can be given from 2-3 weeks of age. One dose only; revaccinate annually
Canine leptospirosis	Usually given in combination with canine distemper vaccine
Canine parvovirus	Usually given in combination with canine distemper vaccination

A properly structured vaccination is essential for each young dog, and this fine litter of Golden Retrievers will benefit from carefully formulated vaccine mixes, given at prescribed intervals.

Inset: A Bulldog bitch with her beautiful puppy, carefully protected against disease by full vaccination.

The breeds

For show purposes, the American Kennel Club divides dogs into six groups: sporting, hounds, working dogs, terriers, toys and non-sporting. Each breed has an official standard of points compiled by breeders and accepted by the American Kennel Club, and it is against this ideal that judges assess dogs of the breed in the show ring.

In this section heights are given to the shoulder or withers, and weights are for the average dog in show condition. For some breeds a particular height or weight is not given, because these are not specified by the AKC.

In order to enhance the alert or fierce expression of some breeds, cosmetic surgery is employed to sharpen the ears by cropping. The American Kennel Club allow for this practice in some types of dog, while in others it would be construed as a disqualifying fault.

POINTER

A good housedog and a fine gundog; affectionate and easily trained; gentle with other pets; good with children; poor watchdog.

Color: Liver, lemon, black, orange, either in combination with white or solid-colored.
Height: Dog 25-28 in; bitch 23-26 in.
Weight: Dog 55-75 lb; bitch 45-65 lb.
Coat type: Short and fine, needs little grooming.
Exercise: Needs a lot, very energetic.

POINTER, GERMAN SHORTHAIRED

A very good housedog and an efficient watchdog; excellent field-dog with keen scenting ability; good with kind children.

Color: Solid liver or any combination of liver and white such as liver and white ticked, liver spotted and white ticked or liver roan.
Height: Dog 23-25 in; bitch 21-23 in.
Weight: Dog 55-70 lb; bitch 45-60 lb.
Coat type: Short and thick; needs regular brushing.
Exercise: Needs a lot; very energetic.

POINTER, GERMAN WIREHAIRED

Good housedog and excellent gundog; can be aggressive; very good watchdog; good with children.

Color: Liver and white, liver and white spotted, liver roan, liver and white spotted with ticking and roaning, solid liver.
Height: Dog 24-26 in; bitch not less than 22 in.
Weight: Dog 60-70 lb; bitch 50-60 lb.
Coat type: Harsh and wiry; needs regular brushing.
Exercise: Needs a lot; very energetic.

Above: The German Wire-Haired Pointer needs a lot of exercise but is good with children and a fine guard.

Below left: Affectionate and easily trained the Pointer is gentle with children and makes a superb gundog.

Below right: Keen scenting ability makes the German Shorthaired Pointer an excellent field dog, and its kind temperament enables it to live happily in the home.

Above left: Often used by police for its superior scenting and tracking abilities, the Labrador Retriever also makes a perfect working dog and family pet.

Above right: After correct training, the Chesapeake Bay Retriever makes a superb gundog, particularly in water. Here this puppy plays with his training lure.

RETRIEVER, CHESAPEAKE BAY
Good gundog, particularly in water; good housedog; quite good with children; inclined to be headstrong and difficult to train; occasionally aggressive.
Color: Any color ranging from dark brown to a faded tan or deadgrass. Deadgrass varies from tan to a dull straw color.
Height: Dog 23-26 in; bitch 21-24 in.
Weight: Dog 65-80 lb; bitch 55-70 lb.
Coat type: Thick and short with dense undercoat, oily and water-resistant; needs normal brushing.
Exercise: Needs lots of hard exercise to maintain condition.

RETRIEVER, CURLY-COATED
Excellent gundog; good family pet; good with children; good watchdog; very kind temperament.
Color: Black or liver.
Height: 25-27 in.
Weight: 70-80 lb.
Coat type: A mass of crisp curls; grooming consists of damping the coat and massaging with fingertips; may require professional trimming.
Exercise: Needs a lot.

RETRIEVER, FLAT-COATED
Very good housedog and an excellent gundog; very good with children; easy to train; very hardy.
Color: Black or liver.
Weight: About 60-70 lb.
Coat type: Dense, fine texture; lying as flat as possible; needs regular brushing.
Exercise: Needs a lot.

RETRIEVER, GOLDEN
Excellent family dog and good gundog; very good with children; poor watchdog; often used as a seeing-eye dog.
Color: Lustrous golden of varying shades.
Height: Dog 23-24 in; bitch 21½-22½ in.
Weight: Dog 65-75 lb; bitch 60-70 lb.
Coat type: Dense and water-repellent, straight or wavy; feathered; needs regular brushing.
Exercise: Needs quite a lot of free (off the leash) exercise.

RETRIEVER, LABRADOR
Excellent family dog and very good gundog; very good with children; poor watchdog; ideal obedience dog; often used by police and armed services.
Color: Black, yellow or chocolate.
Height: Dog 22½-24½ in; bitch 21½-23½ in.
Weight: Dog 60-75 lb; bitch 55-70 lb.
Coat type: Short, dense and hard, no tendency to wave; needs regular grooming.
Exercise: Needs quite a lot of free exercise.

SETTER, ENGLISH

Gentle, loving pet and good gundog; very good with children; poor watchdog; does not like being left alone.

Color: Black, white and tan, black and white, blue belton, lemon and white, lemon belton, orange and white, orange belton, liver and white, liver belton, solid white.

Height: Dog about 25 in; bitch about 24 in.

Weight: Dog about 60-66 lb; bitch about 56-62 lb.

Coat type: Flat and of good length without curl; needs lots of grooming.

Exercise: Needs a lot.

SETTER, GORDON

Affectionate family dog and good gundog; good with children and has an even temperament; poor watchdog.

Color: Black with tan markings.

Height: Dog 24-27 in; bitch 23-26 in.

Weight: Dog 55-80 lb; bitch 45-70 lb.

Coat type: Straight or slightly waved; needs regular grooming.

Exercise: Needs a lot.

Above: The English Setter is a fun-loving, gentle dog which needs a lot of exercise and correct grooming.

Below: The striking black-and-tan Gordon is the largest of the Setters and makes a dignified, even-tempered housepet.

Above: Happy and lively, the Irish Setter needs plenty of exercise each day, along with regular brushing to keep the long, silky coat in good condition.

SETTER, IRISH

Good housedog; excellent gundog; very good with children; poor watchdog.

Color: Mahogany or rich chestnut red.
Height: Dog about 27 in; bitch about 25 in.
Weight: Dog about 70 lb; bitch about 60 lb.
Coat type: Moderately long and silky; feathered; needs regular grooming.
Exercise: Needs a lot.

VIZSLA

One of the world's purest breeds; makes a good family pet; kind temperament; excellent all-purpose gundog; quite good with children; fair watchdog.

Color: Rusty gold to dark sandy yellow; darker shades preferred.
Height: Dog 22-24 in; bitch 21-23 in.
Coat type: Short, smooth and close-lying; needs weekly brushing.
Exercise: Needs lots of hard, vigorous exercise.

Below: Often called the Gray Ghost, the Weimaraner responds well to training for the gun or in obedience.

WEIMARANER

Makes a good housedog unless left to become bored; excellent gundog; good with children; good watchdog; responds very well to training; excels in obedience.

Color: Solid color in shades of mouse-gray to silver-gray.
Height: Dog 25-27 in; bitch 23-25 in.
Coat type: Short, smooth and sleek; needs very little grooming.
Exercise: Needs a great deal to keep fit.

WIREHAIRED POINTING GRIFFON

Basically bred as a working dog; excels as a water dog and retriever; intelligent; loyal; responds readily to training; good-natured.

Color: Steel gray with chestnut splashes, gray-white with chestnut splashes, dirty white with chestnut.
Height: Dog 21½-23½ in; bitch 19½-21½ in.
Coat type: Hard, dry and stiff; regular brushing is needed.
Exercise: Needs a great deal to remain fit.

Below: The russet-colored Vizsla originally came from Hungary and is one of the purest of dog breeds.

An outstanding gundog, it also makes a good pet.

Above: The Cocker Spaniel responds well to training and is excellent as a housedog and with children.

Below: Very popular for Field Trials, the Brittany Spaniel is loyal and sensitive and repays correct training with a high standard of performance.

SPANIEL, AMERICAN WATER

Excellent gundog with outstanding ability as a retriever; fair family dog and an efficient watchdog; responds to training.
Color: Solid liver or dark chocolate.
Height: 15-18 in.
Weight: Dog 28-45 lb; bitch 25-40 lb.
Coat type: Closely curled or with marcel (waved) effect; needs daily brushing and weekly combing; professional stripping may be required.
Exercise: Needs a lot.

SPANIEL, BRITTANY

Good companion and excellent hunter; ideal in field trials; sensitive dog; loyal; responds to correct training.
Color: Orange and white or liver and white in either clear or roan patterns.
Height: 17½-20½ in.
Weight: 30-40 lb.
Coat type: Dense, flat or wavy, not curly; needs daily brushing.
Exercise: Needs a lot.

SPANIEL, CLUMBER

Affectionate and loyal gundog; good with children; responds well to training, fair watchdog.
Color: Lemon and white, orange and white.
Weight: Dog 55-65 lb; bitch 35-50 lb.
Coat type: Dense, silky and straight; feathered; needs regular brushing.
Exercise: Needs lots of free exercise.

SPANIEL, COCKER

An excellent hunter and an affectionate, adaptable housedog; good with children; very responsive to training.
Color: Black variety is jet black; any solid color other than black – any uniform shade; black and tan; parti-color – two or more definite colors in clearly defined markings.
Height: Dog 14½-15½ in; bitch 13½-14½ in.
Coat type: Silky, flat or slightly wavy; needs daily brushing and combing; bath and trim every eight weeks; professional trimming needed at regular intervals.
Exercise: Needs a lot.

SPANIEL, ENGLISH COCKER

Long-lived, gentle housedog and good gundog when correctly trained; excellent with children; poor watchdog.
Color: Various; self-colors; parti-colors; roan in blue, liver, red, orange and lemon.
Height: Dog 16-17 in; bitch 15-16 in.
Weight: Dog 28-34 lb; bitch 26-32 lb.
Coat type: Silky, flat or slightly waved; feathered; needs daily brushing and combing; particular attention must be paid to the ears.
Exercise: Needs regular exercise.

SPANIEL, ENGLISH SPRINGER
Good housedog and excellent field-dog; loyal and intelligent; good with children; poor watchdog.
Color: Black or liver with white markings, white with black or liver markings, black and white or liver and white with tan markings.
Height: Dog 20 in; bitch 19 in.
Weight: Dog 49-55 lb; bitch about 50 lb.
Coat type: Short, close and silky; needs regular grooming.
Exercise: Needs a lot to prevent obesity and skin problems.

SPANIEL, FIELD
Well-balanced dog with a good temperament; excellent fieldworker; docile and affectionate.
Color: Black, liver, golden liver, mahogany red, roan; or any of these colors with tan over the eyes, on the cheeks, feet and pasterns.
Height: About 18 in.
Weight: 35-50 lb.
Coat type: Flat or slightly waved, never curled; silky texture; needs daily grooming to prevent matting.
Exercise: Needs a lot.

Below: Though rather wilful as a puppy, the Welsh Springer Spaniel is very affectionate and makes a good housepet and a superb working dog.

Right: The English Cocker Spaniel has a long history as a working breed. It needs lots of grooming and exercise when kept as a family pet.

SPANIEL, IRISH WATER
Very affectionate, brave and loving housedog; excellent water dog; good watchdog; kind with children.
Color: Solid liver.
Height: Dog 22-24 in; bitch 21-23 in.
Weight: Dog 55-65 lb; bitch 45-58 lb.
Coat type: Densely covered with tight crisp ringlets; needs daily brushing and weekly combing; professional trimming may be required.
Exercise: Needs a great deal.

SPANIEL, SUSSEX
Loyal and undemanding housedog; excellent working dog; good watchdog; quite good with children; very loyal; tends to be a one-man dog.
Color: Rich golden liver.
Height: 15-16 in.
Weight: 35-45 lb.
Coat type: Abundant, flat or slightly waved; daily brushing and combing is necessary, paying particular attention to the ears.
Exercise: Needs lots of long steady exercise.

SPANIEL, WELSH SPRINGER
Good housepet and exceptional gundog; long-lived; affectionate; rather wilful; good with children; poor watchdog.
Color: Dark rich red and white.
Height: Dog 19 in; bitch 18 in.
Coat type: Silky texture, straight, flat and thick; needs regular brushing and combing.
Exercise: Needs a lot of regular steady exercise.

AFGHAN HOUND

Beautiful, glamorous dog; loyal to its own family; good with children unless teased; good guard; can be aloof and independent.
Color: All colors and combinations are acceptable.
Height: Dog 26-28 in; bitch 24-26 in.
Weight: Dog 60 lb; bitch 50 lb.
Coat type: Long; profuse; requiring careful daily grooming.
Exercise: Unrestricted exercise in an enclosed yard is ideal.

BASENJI

Barkless dog with no 'doggy' odor; quiet; gentle; affectionate; thrives as a housedog and is good with children; bitches only come on 'heat' once a year.
Color: Chestnut red, pure black, black and tan, all with white feet, chest and tail tip.
Height: Dog 17 in; bitch 16 in.
Weight: Dog 24 lb; bitch 22 lb.
Coat type: Short and silky with pliant skin; regular use of a hound glove keeps the coat in good condition.
Exercise: Regular long runs needed; a good breed to exercise with horses.

BASSET HOUND

Ideal family pet except for a tendency to wander; even temperament; good with children; good watchdog.
Color: Any recognized hound color and combination.
Height: 14 in.
Coat type: Hard smooth and short; needs daily brushing and regular attention to ears and toenails.
Exercise: Needs a lot.

BEAGLE

Robust, merry and very affectionate; good housedog; fair watchdog; excellent with children; responds to proper training but inclined to wander.
Color: Any true hound color.
Height: Two varieties; thirteen inch – not exceeding 13 in; fifteen inch – 13-15 in.
Coat type: Close hard coat; needs little grooming.
Exercise: Robust and lively; needs unlimited free exercise in yard.

BLACK AND TAN COONHOUND

A true working breed; good temperament; strong and hardy; easily trained; good watchdog.
Color: Coal-black with rich tan markings.
Height: Dog 25-27 in; bitch 23-25 in.
Coat type: Short and very dense; needs regular attention with a hound glove, and attention to ears.
Exercise: Needs lots of vigorous exercise.

BLOODHOUND

Excellent family pet but needs plenty of room; very good with children; very sensitive; responds to quiet careful training; non-aggressive but appearance deters intruders.
Color: Black and tan, red and tan, tawny.
Height: Dog 25-27 in; bitch 23-25 in.
Weight: Dog 90 lb; bitch 80 lb.
Coat type: Short fine coat kept in good condition by regular use of the hound glove; regular attention to ears needed.
Exercise: Needs lots, including a good daily fast run.

Left: The Basenji is unique in being unable to bark. It is a charming little hound, good with children but needs a lot of exercise.

Above: The Beagle seems to wear a perpetual grin and is happy and very affectionate, though it is inclined to wander if the yard gate is left open.

Above left: These Longhaired Miniature Dachshunds are well-loved housepets and make a lot of noise when they hear a stranger's approach.

Above right: Though bred mainly for racing, the retired Greyhound soon adapts to life as a family pet and is good-natured with children, clean and affectionate.

BORZOI

Dignified and good-natured; rather aloof; not good with children; size deters intruders; can be wilful but responds to kind, careful training.
Color: Any color or combination of colors is acceptable.
Height: Dog 28 in; bitch 26 in.
Weight: Dog 75-105 lb; bitch 60-85 lb.
Coat type: Long and silky, either flat, wavy or rather curly; needs regular brushing and combing.
Exercise: Needs a great deal of supervised exercise; keep away from livestock.

DACHSHUND

Bred as a hunting dog, the Dachshund retains its game, courageous nature, but makes a superb housedog, a good watchdog and is excellent with children. Prone to overweight and trouble in the back unless kept fit; rather self-willed.
Color: Red or tan, red-yellow, yellow, brindle; two-colored – deep black, chocolate, gray, and white each with tan markings; dappled – clear brownish or grayish color with dark irregular patches of dark-gray, brown, red-yellow or black.
Weight: Standard – *longhaired* – dog 18 lb; bitch 17 lb; *smooth-haired* – dog 25 lb; bitch 23 lb; *wire-haired* – dog 20-22 lb; bitch 18-20 lb; Miniature (all types) – 10 lb (not exceeding 11 lb).
Coat type: Longhaired – soft sleek, with pronounced feathering; *smoothhaired* – short thick and smooth; *wirehaired* – short, thick, rough, hard coat. the smoothhaired Dachshund needs grooming each day with a hound glove, the longhaired and the wirehaired benefit from a stiff brushing, and a weekly combing.
Exercise: Regular short sharp walks keep this breed in good condition.

FOXHOUND, AMERICAN

Not a pet dog; kept as a show dog and working hound.
Color: Any hound color – black, tan, white in any combination.
Height: Dog 22-25 in; bitch 21-24 in.
Coat type: Close hard hound coat; kept clean with a hound glove.
Exercise: Needs plenty to keep fit.

FOXHOUND, ENGLISH

Not a pet dog; kept as a show dog and working hound.
Color: Any hound color – black, tan, white in any combination.
Height: Dog about 23 in; bitch about 22 in.
Coat type: Close hard hound coat; kept clean with a hound glove.
Exercise: Needs plenty to keep fit.

GREYHOUND

Used mainly for racing, retired Greyhounds make wonderful house pets; good-natured, friendly, affectionate; good with gentle children; may not be reliable with small pets; tends to develop rheumatism and arthritis.
Color: Any color.
Weight: Dog 65-70 lb; bitch 60-65 lb.
Coat type: Short, smooth and firm in texture; keep clean with hound glove; pay attention to toenails.
Exercise: Should not be let off leash; long, steady walks are essential.

Above The Ibizan Hound is a very good-natured dog which gets along with children and other family pets as well as making a fine gundog.

HARRIER
Not a pet breed; remarks as for the Foxhound.
Height: 19-21 in.

IBIZAN HOUND
Excellent housedog; good with children; makes a good gundog; non-aggressive; very sensitive to scolding; needs lots of space; feels the cold.
Color: Red and white, red with white, white with red, lion and white, lion with white, white with lion, solid white, solid red.
Height: Dog 23½-27½ in; bitch 22½-26 in.
Weight: Dog 50 lb; bitch 42-49 lb.
Coat type: Shorthaired – short, close and hard textured; *wirehaired* – up to 3 in long, hard textured. Regular brushing necessary for both coat types.
Exercise: Needs lots of regular steady exercise.

IRISH WOLFHOUND
Superb housedog if given sufficient space; excellent guard dog; good with children; responds to careful training.
Color: Gray, brindle, red, black, pure white, fawn, or Scottish deerhound colors.
Height: Dog 32 in; bitch 30 in.
Weight: Dog 120 lb; bitch 105 lb.
Coat type: Thick and wiry; needs regular brushing; straggling hairs should be plucked out from ears, neck and underside.
Exercise: Needs ample space to allow unlimited free exercise; and long steady walking on the leash.

Left: Twin Otterhound puppies, still lacking the crisp rough coat of the adult, await new owners who will appreciate how much exercise they will need.

Right: One of the best of guard dogs is the loyal and obedient Rhodesian Ridgeback, named after the reversed ridge of hair along its withers.

NORWEGIAN ELKHOUND
Very good housedog; lacks doggy odor; excellent with children; good guard dog; needs firm discipline.
Color: Gray, medium shades preferred.
Height: Dog 20½ in; bitch 19½ in.
Weight: Dog 55 lb; bitch 48 lb.
Coat type: Thick, hard, weather-resisting coat; needs daily brushing and combing.
Exercise: Needs a lot to stay fit.

OTTER HOUND
Amiable and friendly hound; gentle with children; poor watchdog; friendly, but still has the hound temperament.
Colour: Any color or combination of colors.
Height: 24-27 in.
Weight: 75-115 lb.
Coat type: Rough outer coat, 3-6 in deep on back, hard, coarse and crisp; short woolly undercoat; needs thorough brushing and combing right through each week.
Exercise: Needs plenty of exercise.

RHODESIAN RIDGEBACK
Quiet, dignified dog; very affectionate and obedient; very good with children; excellent guard dog; totally loyal.
Color: Light wheaten to red wheaten.
Height: Dog 25-27 in; bitch 24-26 in.
Weight: Dog 75 lb; bitch 65 lb.
Coat type: Short, dense, sleek and glossy; a ridge of hair grows in the opposite direction to the lie of the coat along the withers, giving the dog the impression of having its hackles permanently raised; needs daily grooming with a hound glove.
Exercise: Needs lots of free exercise in an enclosed yard.

Above: The sleek and slender Saluki must have lots of controlled exercise and regular brushing. It is a reliable and intelligent pet and a good watchdog.

SALUKI
Prestigious housedog; excellent guard dog; reliable with children; healthy; intelligent; no doggy odor; should not run free with livestock.
Color: White, fawn, cream, golden, red, grizzle, tan; tricolor – black, white and tan; and black and tan.
Height: Dog 25-28 in; bitch 23-26 in.
Coat type: Smooth soft texture; some feathering; needs daily grooming with a soft brush and a hound glove.
Exercise: Needs a lot of regular exercise.

SCOTTISH DEERHOUND
Imposing, dignified pet; loving and intelligent; needs a lot of space; responds to careful, sensitive training.
Color: Dark blue-gray, dark and light brindles, yellow and sand red, red-fawn.
Height: Dog 30-32 in; bitch about 28 in or more.
Weight: Dog 85-110 lb; bitch 75-95 lb.
Coat type: Harsh and wiry; needs regular brushing; untidy hairs may be plucked out with the thumb and forefinger.
Exercise: Needs plenty to remain fit.

WHIPPET
Perfect housedog and excellent sporting dog; clean; affectionate; very good with children; has strong hunting instincts.
Color: Any color acceptable.
Height: Dog 19-22 in; bitch 18-21 in.
Coat type: Close, smooth and firm texture coat; needs occasional use of the hound glove and regular attention to ears and toenails.
Exercise: A racing breed, therefore needs lots of fast work to keep really fit.

Group III: Working dogs

AKITA
Good-natured and affectionate; excellent with children and as a guard dog; intelligent and easily trained.
Color: Any color including white, brindle and pinto.
Height: Dog 26-28 in; bitch 24-26 in.
Coat type: Double coat – undercoat soft and dense, outer coat harsh and weatherproof; needs daily brushing.
Exercise: Needs only a little exercise.

ALASKAN MALAMUTE
Mainly used as a sled-dog, but is good with the family and protective towards children; affectionate, strong and very fast.
Color: Ranges from light-gray through intermediate shades to black, with white underbody, and some white around the face.
Height: Dog 25 in; bitch 23 in.
Weight: Dog 85 lb; bitch 75 lb.
Coat type: Thick coarse guard (top) coat, soft dense undercoat; woollie and oily; needs regular brushing.
Exercise: Needs a lot of fast work.

BEARDED COLLIE
Playful and very intelligent; loves children; can be protective; inclined to 'herd' other pets.
Color: The Bearded Collie is born either black, blue, brown or fawn, and lightens with maturity; tan markings occasionally appear.
Height: Dog 21-22 in; bitch 20-21 in.
Coat type: Double coat – harsh shaggy top coat, soft furry undercoat; needs daily brushing and occasional bathing and chalking.
Exercise: Needs a lot of exercise.

BELGIAN MALINOIS
Robust; alert and intelligent; responds well to correct training; excellent guard dog; good with children.
Color: Rich fawn to mahogany with black overlay, mask and ears.
Height: Dog 24-26 in; bitch 22-24 in.
Coat type: Short, straight with dense undercoat; needs only occasional brushing; combing removes the undercoat.
Exercise: Needs regular steady walking.

BELGIAN SHEEPDOG
Ideal companion and guard dog; very intelligent and has been used as a war dog; responds to careful training; rather sensitive.
Color: Black, or black with limited white markings.
Height: Dog 24-26 in; bitch 22-24 in.
Coat type: Medium-hard straight top coat; dense undercoat; needs occasional brushing; combing removes the undercoat.
Exercise: Needs regular steady work.

Above: Though it was primarily developed as a sled-dog, the Alaskan Malamute is popular as an impressive guard, and is good with children.

Left: The Bearded Collie or 'Beardie' loves children and, despite its need for regular grooming and plenty of exercise, is a popular pet.

Above left: The Boxer is a fine guard but may be inclined to fight with other dogs. It needs a lot of exercise but very little grooming to keep its short coat in order.

Above right: Although it is rather sensitive and needs careful training, the Belgian Tervuren is intelligent and very affectionate, particularly towards children in the family.

BELGIAN TERVUREN

Intelligent and affectionate; makes excellent guard dog and is protective to children in the family; responds well to careful training; rather sensitive.
Color: Rich fawn to mahogany with black overlay; each hair tipped with black; black mask and ears.
Height: Dog 24-26 in; bitch 22-24 in.
Coat type: Hard, straight and abundant top coat; dense undercoat; needs occasional brushing; combing removes undercoat.
Exercise: Needs regular steady work.

BERNESE MOUNTAIN DOG

Excellent housedog if sufficient space; very good with children and with other pets; good guard dog; easily trained.
Color: Jet-black with russet-brown or deep-tan markings.
Height: Dog 23-27½ in; bitch 21-26 in.
Coat type: Soft and silky, long and slightly wavy; needs regular brushing.
Exercise: Needs quite a lot to keep healthy.

BOUVIER DES FLANDRES

One-man dog; excellent guard dog – can be very fierce; trustworthy and loyal to own family; responds well to proper training.
Color: From fawn to black, passing through salt and pepper, gray and brindle.
Height: Dog 24½-27½ in; bitch 23½-26½ in.
Coat type: Tousled double coat – harsh top coat, soft undercoat; regular brushing keeps coat tidy.
Exercise: Needs a lot to keep fit and contented.

BOXER

Happy-natured housedog; good guard dog; wonderful with children; loyal; inclined to fight; needs correct training and a spacious home.
Color: Fawn and brindle.
Height: Dog 22½-25 in; bitch 21-23½ in.
Coat type: Short and smooth; needs a light brush every day.
Exercise: Needs quite a lot of supervised exercise.

BRIARD

Ideal family pet and farm worker/herder; gentle and easy to train; can be over-protective.
Color: All uniform colors except white.
Height: Dog 23-27 in; bitch 22-25½ in.
Coat type: Outer coat is hard, coarse and dry, undercoat fine and tight; needs regular brushing.
Exercise: Regular steady work is essential.

BULLMASTIFF

Lovable and trustworthy if properly reared and trained; loyal and affectionate; superlative guard dog; good with own family's children; needs plenty of room.

Color: Red, fawn and brindle.
Height: Dog 25-27 in; bitch 24-26 in.
Weight: Dog 110-130 lb; bitch 100-120 lb.
Coat type: Short and dense; needs occasional brushing.
Exercise: Regular steady exercise is required.

COLLIE

Very responsive to training; makes good obedience dog; very good with children; good watchdog; loyal and affectionate.

Color: Sable and white; tri-color (black with white markings and tan shadings); blue merle (mottled or marbled blue-gray and black, with white markings); and white (white with sable, tri-color or blue-merle markings).
Height: Dog 24-26 in; bitch 22-24 in.
Weight: Dog 60-75 lb; bitch 50-65 lb.
Coat type: Rough Collie – abundant, except on head and legs; outer coat is straight and harsh to touch, undercoat soft and furry. Smooth Collie – short, hard and dense flat coat of good texture, with an abundant short undercoat. Both types of Collie require thorough grooming to keep the coat clean and fresh; the Rough Collie needs extra attention to the underbody and inside of the legs.
Exercise: Needs regular steady exercise.

Above: Obedient, loyal and affectionate, Rough Collies like these make good family dogs, but need lots of grooming and plenty of exercise.

Above: The Giant Schnauzer makes an unusual pet. He is an outstanding guard, being totally fearless and disliking strangers, but is protective towards children.

DOBERMANN PINSCHER

Superlative guard dog; brave, loyal and intelligent; must be properly trained from an early age; can be wilful; very good with own family's children and other pets; needs space.

Color: Black, red, blue and fawn (Isabella); all with sharply defined rust markings.
Height: Dog 26-28 in; bitch 24-26 in.
Coat type: Smooth-haired, short, close-lying; needs occasional rub-down with a hound glove or rough towel.
Exercise: Very energetic; needs lots of exercise to keep fit.

GERMAN SHEPHERD DOG (ALSATIAN)

Excellent housedog and ideal guard dog; trains well and is ideal for obedience work; favored as police and army dog; needs knowledgeable handing from puppyhood; highly intelligent.

Color: Most colors are permitted, strong rich colors preferred.
Height: Dog 24-26 in; bitch 22-24 in.
Coat type: Double coat of medium length; needs daily brushing.
Exercise: Needs a lot to stay healthy and prevent boredom.

GIANT SCHNAUZER

Good-natured and playful; totally fearless and an excellent guard dog; very protective with children and family; wary of strangers.

Color: Solid black or pepper and salt.
Height: Dog 25½-27½ in; bitch 23½-25½ in.
Coat type: Hard, wiry and very dense; needs daily grooming with a wire brush, regular stripping or plucking and daily combing of the muzzle hair.
Exercise: Needs a lot of exercise.

Above left: Another fine guard dog is the Kuvasz, which is loyal and protective towards its own family. The white double coat needs a thorough daily brushing.

Above right: The Komondor is another white colored breed with an unusual coat which forms long cords. It is hardy and good with the family but makes a fierce guard.

GREAT DANE

Good-natured and easily trained family dog; needs plenty of space for living; gets on well with other pets; good with children; not particularly fierce but size deters intruders; rather short-lived.
Color: Brindle, fawn, blue, black, harlequin (white with black patches).
Height: Dog at least 30 in; bitch at least 28 in.
Coat type: Short, thick, smooth and glossy; needs daily grooming with the correct brush; must have a warm comfortable bed with protection from the pressure points.
Exercise: Short regular periods of exercise on hard ground are needed.

GREAT PYRENEES

Good housedog if given sufficient space; excellent guard dog; good with other pets; easily trained; lives happily out of doors.
Color: White or principally white with badger, gray or tan markings.
Height: Dog 27-32 in; bitch 25-29 in.
Weight: Dog 100-125 lb; bitch 90-115 lb.
Coat type: Long, thick, coarse outer coat; heavy, fine undercoat; needs very regular brushing to keep it in good condition.
Exercise: Normal steady walking needed.

KOMONDOR

Very loyal family dog; ferocious guard dog; good with own family's pets and children; lives equally well indoors or out; unusual corded coat rarely sheds.
Color: White.
Height: Dog 25½ in; bitch 23½ in.
Coat type: Dense, weather-resistant double coat; tassel-like cords form naturally; occasional washing keeps the cords clean and fresh; never brushed or combed.
Exercise: Needs a moderate amount.

KUVASZ

Outstanding guard dog; loyal and protective to own family; responds to careful training; very sensitive.
Color: White.
Height: Dog 28-30 in; bitch 26-28 in.
Weight: Dog 100-115 lb; bitch 70-90 lb.
Coat type: Double coat of medium-coarse texture; straight or wavy; needs regular, thorough brushing.
Exercise: Needs a lot to stay fit.

MASTIFF

Dignified, loyal and intelligent; superb guard dog; good family dog if given sufficient space; good with own family's pets and children.
Color: Apricot, silver, fawn or dark-fawn to brindle.
Height: Dog at least 30 in; bitch at least 27½ in.
Coat type: Coarse top coat, short dense and close-lying undercoat; regular brushing keeps the coat clean and healthy.
Exercise: Regular steady walking, or free exercise in enclosed yard needed.

NEWFOUNDLAND

Exceptional family dog but needs sufficient space; good guard dog; responds to careful training; superb swimmer.

Color: Black, or black with some white markings; bronze with some white markings; Landseer white with black markings.
Height: Dog 28 in; bitch 26 in.
Weight: Dog 150 lb; bitch 120 lb.
Coat type: Water-resistant double coat, long and full without curl; needs grooming daily with a hard brush.
Exercise: Regular steady work on hard ground needed.

OLD ENGLISH SHEEPDOG

Loyal and affectionate; good housedog if given sufficient room; excellent with own family's children and other pets.

Color: Any shade of gray, grizzle, blue or blue-merle.
Height: Dog at least 22 in; bitch slightly smaller.
Coat type: Profuse, but not excessive; hard, shaggy and free from curl; needs daily brushing and weekly combing; special attention required for ears, hair between toes and over the face; occasional chalking needed.
Exercise: Needs a lot, including free exercise.

PULI

Very loyal, a one-man dog; natural herder; excellent guard dog; good with own family's children and pets; responds well to correct training.

Color: Black, rusty-black, various shades of gray, white.
Height: Dog 17-19 in; bitch 16-18 in.
Coat type: Dense double coat; outer coat is long and of medium texture, may be combed or corded; corded coats need to be regularly washed and carefully dried.
Exercise: Needs plenty of exercise.

Above: This big dog called the Newfoundland was developed for work in water and has a thick water-resistant coat. It makes an exceptional family dog and guard.

ROTTWEILER

Good family dog; has been used by police, as a sled-dog and for mountain rescue; exceptional guard dog; loyal; affectionate; needs correct training.

Color: Black with clearly defined tan or mahogany markings.
Height: Dog 24-27 in; bitch 22-26 in.
Coat type: Short, coarse and flat; needs light regular brushing.
Exercise: Needs regular steady work.

SAINT BERNARD

Loyal and affectionate; superb family dog when given sufficient space; very intelligent and easy to train; short-lived.

Color: White with red or red with white.
Height: Dog at least 27½ in; bitch at least 25½ in.
Coat type: Shorthaired – dense, short, lying smooth; *longhaired* – medium length, wavy. Daily brushing is required for both types of coat.
Exercise: Needs only short walks and some free exercise in an enclosed yard.

SAMOYED

Rather independent; intelligent; responds to careful training; devoted to owner; quite effective as a watchdog.

Color: White, white and biscuit, cream, biscuit.
Height: Dog 21-23½ in; bitch 19-21 in.
Coat type: Double-coated – top coat long and hard, undercoat soft, short, thick, close wool; very regular brushing and combing is needed; must be toweled dry when wet; undercoat sheds and bathing helps to loosen the coat at this time.
Exercise: Needs lots of exercise.

Above: A good all-rounder, the Rottweiler must have correct training as a juvenile in order to make a reliable pet. It is an excellent guard, with an easy-care coat.

Above: The Samoyed can be wilful but will respond to careful training and soon becomes devoted to a kind owner. The light coat sheds and needs regular brushing.

SHETLAND SHEEPDOG

Good family dog; wary of strangers; highly intelligent; responds well to training and makes an excellent obedience dog; good with own family's children and pets.

Color: Black, blue-merle, sable; marked with varying amounts of white and/or tan.

Height: 13-16 in.

Coat type: Double-coat – outer coat long, straight and harsh, undercoat short, furry and very dense; use a stiff brush every day; comb behind the ears, on the underbody and between the legs.

Exercise: Free exercise in an enclosed yard is sufficient.

SIBERIAN HUSKY

Typical sled dog; good family dog; protective and loyal; good with own family's children; friendly and adaptable.

Color: All colors from black to white with a variety of head markings.

Height: Dog 21-23½ in; bitch 20-22 in.

Weight: Dog 45-60 lb; bitch 35-50 lb.

Coat type: Double-coat; medium in length; needs regular brushing.

Exercise: Needs a lot of exercise or becomes bored and obese.

STANDARD SCHNAUZER

Excellent guard dog; dislikes strangers; affectionate; lively and playful; good with own family's children.

Color: Pepper and salt or pure black.

Height: Dog 18½-19½ in; bitch 17½-18½ in.

Coat type: Tight, hard and wiry; brush every day; professional trimming required at regular intervals.

Exercise: Regular steady exercise required.

WELSH CORGI – CARDIGAN

Quiet, hardy housedog; very good with children; excellent guard dog.

Color: All shades of red; all shades of brindle; black, with or without tan or brindle points; blue-merle with or without tan or brindle points.

Height: About 12 in.

Coat type: Medium length; dense; the coat requires daily brushing.

Exercise: Regular daily exercise is essential to prevent obesity.

WELSH CORGI – PEMBROKE

Hardy, tireless and happy housedog; excellent guard dog; good with children; responds well to correct training; dislikes strangers.

Color: Red, sable, fawn, black and tan; all with or without white markings.

Height: 10-12 in.

Weight: 25-27 lb.

Coat type: Medium length, short and thick; daily brushing is essential.

Exercise: Moderate amounts of exercise are required to prevent obesity.

Above: Saint Bernard dogs need lots of space in which to take free exercise. They are loyal and affectionate to their own family but often dislike strangers.

61

Group IV: Terriers

TERRIER, AIREDALE

Excellent family dog and guard; very good with own family's children; sound temperament; called the King of Terriers.

Color: Tan with darker ears; black markings on the sides and saddle.

Height: Dog 23 in; bitch 22 in.

Coat type: Hard dense and wiry; needs grooming with stiff brush every day and regular hand-stripping to keep coat neat.

Exercise: Needs a lot to keep fit; ideal dog to exercise with horses.

TERRIER, AMERICAN STAFFORDSHIRE

Totally fearless; excellent guard; protective with children; likes to scrap; can be stubborn; needs proper training.

Color: Any color: solid, parti or patched.

Height: Dog 18-19 in; bitch 17-18 in.

Coat type: Short, close, stiff to touch; regular brushing needed.

Exercise: Needs regular walks, and free exercise in enclosed yard.

TERRIER, AUSTRALIAN

Alert and happy housedog; loves children; enjoys a scrap; not good with other pets; good watchdog.

Color: Blue-black or silver-black with rich tan markings; sandy or clear red.

Height: About 10 in.

Weight: 10-12 lb.

Coat type: Harsh and straight with soft undercoat; needs regular grooming with a stiff bristle brush and occasional bathing.

Exercise: Needs a surprising amount; must be controlled or may fight.

TERRIER, BEDLINGTON

Excellent watchdog; loves children; well behaved in the home; needs very careful training.

Color: Blue, sandy, liver, blue and tan, sandy and tan, liver and tan.

Height: Dog 16½ in; bitch 15½ in.

Weight: 17-23 lb.

Coat type: Distinctive mixture of hard and soft hair; crisp with tendency to curl; never sheds; pluck untidy hair; trim regularly.

Exercise: Needs regular steady work.

Left: Airedale Terriers make perfect guards and are protective towards their own family's children. The dense wiry coat needs regular stripping to stay tidy.

Above: A Smooth-Coated Fox Terrier makes a good watchdog and a clean obedient housepet needing little grooming but lots of free exercise in an enclosed yard.

TERRIER, BORDER

Very even-natured, hardy housedog; good with children and other pets; responds well to training.
Color: Red, grizzle and tan, blue and tan or wheaten.
Weight: Dog 13-15½ lb; bitch 11½-14 lb.
Coat type: Dense undercoat, wiry top coat; needs occasional trimming and very occasional brushing.
Exercise: Needs a lot of regular exercise to keep fit.

TERRIER, BULL

Superb with children; excellent guard dog; affectionate and intelligent; needs early disciplining.
Color: White – white, but may have colored markings on the head; *colored* – any color other than white, or any color with white markings.
Coat type: Short, flat and harsh to the touch; needs normal daily brushing only.
Exercise: Controlled exercise is essential as this breed enjoys a fight; free exercise in an enclosed yard is ideal.

TERRIER, CAIRN

Ideal family dog; good with children and other pets; hardy, healthy and affectionate; very energetic.
Color: Any color except white.
Height: Dog 10 in; bitch 9½ in.
Weight: Dog 14 lb; bitch 13 lb.
Coat type: Hard, weather-resistant; double with harsh top coat and soft undercoat; requires daily brushing, with underparts combed; remove long hairs from ears and underbody, and trim away any feathering.
Exercise: Needs plenty of controlled exercise to keep fit.

TERRIER, DANDIE DINMONT

One-man dog which makes an excellent watchdog; courageous and intelligent; not good with children or with other pets.
Color: Pepper or mustard.
Height: 8-11 in.
Weight: 18-24 lb.
Coat type: A mixture of hard and soft hair about 2 in in length, giving a crisp feel; needs grooming with a stiff brush; old or straggly hairs should be hand-plucked.
Exercise: Needs a lot of exercise to keep fit.

TERRIER, FOX

Alert and very lively housedog; good watchdog; good with own family's children; needs careful training.
Color: White should predominate, brindle, red or liver markings are objectionable.
Height: Up to 15½ in.
Weight: 18 lb.
Coat type: Smooth – smooth, flat and hard; needs daily brushing and very occasional trimming away of straggly hair; chalk white areas; *Wirehair* – hard and wiry; hand-stripping is necessary at quarterly intervals and for showing; watch the skin for eczema; brush carefully each day; chalk white areas.
Exercise: Needs a lot of controlled exercise and free running in an enclosed area.

Above: Though the Irish Terrier likes nothing better than a good fight with other dogs, it is a happy natured pet and very faithful to its family and friends.

TERRIER, IRISH

Excellent family dog and good watchdog; alert and easily trained with kindness; loves to fight; very faithful.
Color: Bright red, golden red, red wheaten, wheaten.
Height: About 18 in.
Weight: About 27 lb.
Coat type: Dense and wiry; needs hand-stripping at regular intervals as well as daily brushing.
Exercise: Needs lots of controlled exercise; avoid other animals.

TERRIER, KERRY BLUE

Good house pet and excellent guard dog; good with own family's children; not good with other pets; needs very careful training; enjoys fighting.
Color: Any shade of blue-gray or gray-blue.
Height: Dog 18-19½ in; bitch 17½-19 in.
Coat type: Soft, dense and wavy; needs daily brushing; comb longer hairs; regular trimming required.
Exercise: Needs a lot of exercise.

TERRIER, LAKELAND

Good family dog; excellent with children; very good guard dog; intelligent and easily trained; very lively and energetic.

Color: Blue, black, liver, black and tan, blue and tan, red, red grizzle, grizzle and tan, wheaten.
Height: Dog 14½ in; bitch 13½ in.
Coat type: Hard and wiry with a soft undercoat; needs daily brushing and regular professional trimming.
Exercise: Needs a great deal to stay fit.

TERRIER, MANCHESTER

A well-balanced and adaptable family dog; long-lived; very clean in habits; calm and responds well to training.

Color: Jet black and rich mahogany tan.
Weight: Toy variety – not exceeding 12 lb; *standard variety* – over 12 lb, not exceeding 22 lb.
Coat type: Smooth, short, dense and close; brush daily; towel dry when wet.
Exercise: Needs moderate, regular exercise.

SCHNAUZER, MINIATURE

Happy and alert family dog; excellent guard dog; good with own family's children; responds well to early training; makes a good obedience dog.

Color: Salt and pepper, black and silver, solid black.
Height: 12-14 in.
Coat type: Harsh and wiry with soft undercoat; brush weekly to remove dead hair; needs regular hand-stripping.
Exercise: Needs regular steady exercise.

TERRIER, NORFOLK

Gay, adaptable family dog; very good with children; equable temperament; responds well to training.

Color: All shades of red, red wheaten, black and tan, grizzle.
Height: 10 in.
Weight: 10-12 lb.
Coat type: Hard, wiry and straight; needs only occasional grooming.
Exercise: Likes quite a lot.

TERRIER, NORWICH

Good family dog; excellent with children; intelligent and easily trained; lively and energetic.

Color: All shades of red, wheaten, black and tan, grizzle.
Height: 10 in.
Weight: 11-12 lb.
Coat type: Hard and wiry; needs very little grooming or trimming.
Exercise: Likes a lot, but can make do with less.

TERRIER, SCOTTISH

Good housedog and brave guard dog; not good with small children; enjoys a fight; very loyal and responds well to training.

Color: Steel or iron gray, brindled or grizzled, black, sandy or wheaten.
Height: Dog 10 in; bitch 10 in.
Weight: Dog 19-22 lb; bitch 18-21 lb.
Coat type: Hard and wiry with dense undercoat.
Exercise: Needs unlimited free exercise in enclosed yard.

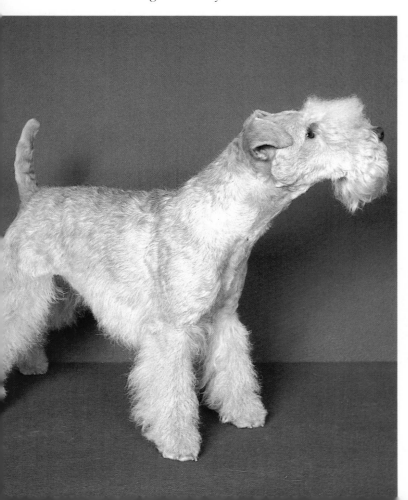

Left: This beautiful Lakeland Terrier shows the results of expert trimming and grooming ready for the show ring.

Above: Usually under 10in in height, the Skye Terrier is shy but very affectionate with members of his own family. The long coat needs daily combing to remain tidy.

TERRIER, SEALYHAM

Devoted and loyal housedog; good with children; can be stubborn and obstinate unless correctly trained; enjoys a fight.

Color: All white, or white with lemon, tan or badger markings on the head.
Height: 10½ in.
Weight: About 23-24 lb.
Coat type: Hard and wiry with a soft dense undercoat; needs hand-stripping twice a year and regular grooming with a wire comb.
Exercise: Likes quite a lot, but can make do with less.

TERRIER, SKYE

Rather shy of strangers; loyal and affectionate housedog; quiet and patient temperament; needs careful training.

Color: Black, blue, dark or light gray, silver-platinum, fawn or cream.
Height: Dog 10 in; bitch 9½ in.
Coat type: Hard, straight top coat 5½ in. long; soft, short undercoat; brush daily and comb weekly with a wide-toothed comb.
Exercise: Likes a lot, but can make do with less.

TERRIER, SOFT-COATED WHEATEN

Sweet-natured dog; excellent with children; defensive without being aggressive; intelligent; easy to train; undemanding.

Color: Wheaten.
Height: Dog 18-19 in; bitch 17-18 in.
Weight: Dog 35-45 lb; bitch 30-40 lb.
Coat type: Abundant, soft and wavy; does not shed; groom only with a medium-toothed comb; bath when necessary; pluck straggly hairs from the body.
Exercise: Likes a lot of exercise.

TERRIER, STAFFORDSHIRE BULL

Sound, excellent family dog; fearless and a good guard; rather stubborn and needs careful early training.

Color: Red, fawn, white, black, blue, or any of these colors with white; any shade of brindle or brindle with white.
Height: 14-16 in.
Weight: Dog 28-38 lb; bitch 24-34 lb.
Coat type: Smooth, short and close-lying; never trimmed; brush from time to time.
Exercise: Likes a fight so must be exercised on the leash.

TERRIER, WELSH

Good housedog with an even temperament; bold and lively; full of fun; playful and affectionate; quite good with children.

Color: Black and tan, black grizzle and tan.
Height: Dog 15 in; bitch 14 in.
Coat type: Wiry, hard, close and abundant; needs hand-stripping twice a year and regular brushing.
Exercise: Like a lot, but can make do with less.

TERRIER, WEST HIGHLAND WHITE

Hardy, happy housedog; good with children and other pets; very easy to train and eager to please.

Color: White.
Height: Dog 11 in; bitch 10 in.
Coat type: Outer coat of straight hard hair, undercoat soft; needs brushing and combing every day and hand-stripping twice a year; remove straggly hairs by plucking the neckline, ears and tail.
Exercise: Likes a lot but can make do with less.

AFFENPINSCHER
Appealing little dog with a comical, monkey-like face; brave and a good watchdog; very affectionate.
Color: Black, black with tan, red, gray and other colors.
Height: 9½-11 in.
Weight: 6½-9 lb.
Coat type: Short, dense and shaggy in parts, coarse and wiry in others; needs regular brushing.
Exercise: Needs only short walks.

BRUSSELS GRIFFON
Attractive happy little dog, with a monkey-like face; long-lived and obedient; hardy and intelligent.
Color: Rough-coated – reddish-brown, black and reddish-brown, black with uniform reddish-brown markings; *smooth-coated* – same as rough-coated except that black is not allowed.
Weight: 8-10 lb.
Coat type: Rough-coated – wiry and dense; regular brushing and hand-stripping twice a year are needed; *smooth-coated* – brush gently then smooth with a towel or piece of velvet; keep the toenails clipped.
Exercise: Likes a romp, but is undemanding.

Above: This tiny little dog with the cute expression is an Affenpinscher, and despite his diminutive height is fearless and makes an excellent watchdog.

Below: Another small dog with a monkey-like face is the Brussels Griffon, which is long-lived, obedient and easily trained as an undemanding family pet.

CHIHUAHUA
Good family dog; excellent with children; good guard dog; intelligent and easily trained; lively, energetic.
Color: Any color, solid, marked or splashed.
Weight: Not over 6 lb.
Coat type: Smooth-coated – soft texture, close-lying; groom with a soft brush and polish with a velvet pad; clip toenails; *long-coated* – soft texture, flat or wavy, with undercoat; brush daily and polish with a velvet pad; clip toenails; check ears.
Exercise: Very little exercise required.

ENGLISH TOY SPANIEL
Wonderful housedog; excellent with children; gets on well with other pets; hardy and affectionate.
Color: The King Charles and Ruby are solid-color dogs; King Charles are black and tan; Ruby are a rich chestnut-red. Blenheim and Prince Charles are broken-color dogs; the Blenheim is red and white; the Prince Charles is white, black and tan.
Weight: 9-12 lb.
Coat type: Long, silky, soft and wavy; needs regular brushing with a bristle brush; watch ears for signs of ear mites and toes for interdigital cysts; keep eyes clean with a saline solution, applied with cotton buds.
Exercise: Enjoys regular walks.

ITALIAN GREYHOUND
Ideal housedog; clean, odor-free and very obedient; affectionate and easy to train; rarely molts.
Color: Any color except tan or brindle markings.
Height: 13-15 in.
Coat type: Very short and soft; rub coat with a silk scarf or velvet pad; pay attention to ears, teeth and toenails.
Exercise: Enjoys a good run but must be protected from the cold and wet.

Above left: The petite Japanese Chin has a merry nature and is loyal and obedient. It loves children and other pet animals and enjoys having attention paid to its profuse coat.

Above right: The beautiful satin-like coat of the Italian Greyhound needs little care and stays clean and odor-free at all times. This breed is extremely affectionate and loyal.

JAPANESE CHIN

Happy and hardy housedog; good with children and other pets; loyal and affectionate; eager to please.
Color: Black and white or red and white.
Weight: 4-7 lb.
Coat type: Profuse, long and straight; needs daily attention with a bristle brush and occasional bathing.
Exercise: Loves a good run but must not be allowed to overtire itself.

MALTESE

Even-tempered, healthy dog; long-lived; very good with children and other pets; responds to careful training.
Color: Pure white; light tan or lemon is allowed on ears.
Weight: 4-6 lb.
Coat type: Single textured, long and silky; groom with a bristle brush every day from early puppyhood; use baby powder to separate hair; bath regularly.
Exercise: Enjoys a good romp.

Above: The long silky coat of the Maltese requires brushing every day from early puppyhood plus regular bathing. This breed is very good with children, affectionate and hardy.

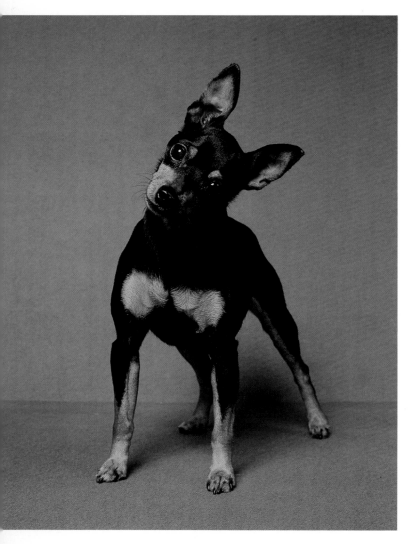

MINIATURE PINSCHER
Good housedog; fearless and easy to care for; intelligent and easily trained; not good with children or other pets.
Color: Solid red, stag red, black and tan.
Height: 11-11½ in.
Coat type: Smooth, hard and very short; needs daily grooming with a soft brush and a rub down with a velvet pad or silk scarf.
Exercise: Needs very little but enjoys a romp.

PAPILLON
The Butterfly Dog, named after its large fringed ears; affectionate and obedient; possessive towards owner; can be jealous.
Color: Always parti-color, white with patches of any color.
Height: 8-11 in.
Coat type: Abundant, long and flowing; needs daily grooming.
Exercise: Enjoys a run but is undemanding.

PEKINGESE
Very brave little dog; loyal and affectionate; not good with children or other pets; generally healthy and long-lived; may be prone to eye trouble.
Color: Red, fawn, black, black and tan, sable, brindle, white and part-colors.
Weight: Not more than 14 lb.
Coat type: Long, straight and flat with thick undercoat; groom daily with soft bristle brush, paying attention to the underbody and using baby powder to separate the hair; bathing is rarely necessary.
Exercise: Should not be overexerted or overheated; steady walking for short distances is sufficient.

Above: Though small in stature, the Miniature Pinscher makes a good watchdog, warning of the approach of strangers with a strong bark. It is easily trained and intelligent.

Below: The Papillon is affectionate and obedient with its owner but may exhibit a jealous nature within the family circle. Its abundant flowing coat needs daily grooming.

PUG
Charming family pet; very good with children; intelligent and affectionate; responds to careful training.
Color: Silver or apricot-fawn.
Weight: 14-18 lb.
Coat type: Fine, smooth, soft and short; brush through daily.
Exercise: Take care not to overexert or overheat; gentle walking on the leash and attention to a correct diet will aid fitness.

SHIH TZU
Happy and affectionate housedog; excellent with children; very intelligent and responds to careful training.
Color: All colors permissible.
Height: 9-11½ in.
Weight: 12-15 lb.
Coat type: Luxurious long and dense coat; must be groomed every day with a pure bristle brush to prevent formation of mats and tangles; check ears and tie up top-knot to protect the eyes.
Exercise: Needs short, regular walks, and enjoys a good romp.

Above: This lovely little Pekingese is living up to his breed reputation of expecting every home comfort to be provided by his doting owners, and takes the best chair.

Right: The minute Yorkshire Terrier generally imagines himself to be a much larger breed and is totally fearless in his defence of his owners, property and home.

TERRIER, SILKY

Dainty little housedog; alert and affectionate; very hardy; responds well to careful training.

Color: Blue and tan.
Weight: 8-10 lb.
Coat type: Fine texture, long and silky; brush through every day; comb weekly; bath regularly.
Exercise: Enjoys a good run.

TERRIER, YORKSHIRE

Happy housedog; good watchdog; affectionate, healthy and quite fearless; good with children and other pets.

Color: Puppies are born black and tan; adult dogs are blue and tan.
Weight: Not above 7 lb.
Coat type: Long, fine and silky; regular brushing, combing and oiling is required to keep the coat in good condition.
Exercise: Likes long walks, but is undemanding.

BICHON FRISE
Appealing and happy housedog; a good pet; good with children and other pets; responds to careful training.
Color: Solid white or white with cream, apricot, or gray markings, on ears and/or body.
Height: 8-12 in.
Coat type: Profuse, silky and loosely curled; needs expert trimming and very regular brushing and combing.
Exercise: Enjoys leash walking and free exercise.

BOSTON TERRIER
Affectionate and intelligent; excellent housedog and good with children and other pets; rarely sheds hairs; odorless; dislikes cold and damp.
Color: Brindle with white markings; black with white markings allowed.
Weight: Lightweight – under 15 lb; *middleweight* – 15-20 lb; *heavyweight* – 20-25 lb.
Coat type: Short, smooth and fine texture; daily brushing required.
Exercise: Likes a daily walk.

Left: With its loosely curled coat and naturally smiling face the Bichon Frise is an appealing pet, good with other animals and small children, and very affectionate.

Below left: Boston Terriers are fond of company and dislike cold and damp. The short smooth coat rarely sheds hair in the home and needs only a minimum of brushing each day.

BULLDOG

Good watchdog; happy and loyal housedog; good-natured and very good with children and other pets; inclined to snore.
Color: Red brindle, other brindles, solid white, solid red, fawn or fallow, piebald.
Weight: Dog 50 lb; bitch 40 lb.
Coat type: Straight, short and flat; daily rubdown with a hound glove keeps the coat in good condition.
Exercise: Avoid exertion.

CHOW CHOW

One-man dog; loyal and affectionate; not good with children or other pets; dislikes strangers; odor-free.
Color: Any clear color.
Height: At least 18 in.
Coat type: Abundant, dense, straight and off-standing; needs 5 to 10 minutes' brushing every day, and an hour each week with a wire brush.
Exercise: Needs a lot of hard exercise on firm ground.

DALMATIAN

Happy and unusual dog; good with children and other dogs; easily trained; generally long-lived; coat sheds throughout the year.
Color: White with dense black spots or liver-brown spots; the spots must be as round and well-defined as possible, varying in size from a dime to a half-dollar.
Height: 19-23 in.
Coat type: Short, hard, dense and sleek; needs daily brushing and regular bathing.
Exercise: Bred to run with horse and carriage, this breed requires considerable exercise to remain fit.

FRENCH BULLDOG

Ideal family dog; loves children; very affectionate and eager to please; responds well to careful training.
Color: All brindle, fawn, white, brindle and white, pied and fawn.
Weight: Lightweight – up to 22 lb; *heavyweight* – 22-28 lb.
Coat type: Fine, short and smooth; needs normal daily brushing.
Exercise: Needs short, regular walks, and free exercise in an enclosed yard.

KEESHOND

One-man dog; excellent watchdog; long-lived; good temperament; responds to careful training; quiet and unobtrusive.
Color: A mixture of gray and black.
Height: Dog 18 in; bitch 17 in.
Coat type: Abundant, long, straight, harsh hair outstanding; needs daily grooming with stiff brush.
Exercise: Requires moderate exercise.

Left: The typical Bulldog is happy, affectionate and loyal to his owners, and very good with children and other pets. He requires little exercise.

Above: A true Spitz, the Chow Chow dislikes strangers, but is fiercely loyal to his own family. An interesting feature of the breed is its unusual black tongue.

Below: The French Bulldog proves amenable to early training and soon becomes an ideal family dog, good with small children and always ready for a game or a walk.

Above: The Lhasa Apso was considered the most coveted gift that could be bestowed by the Dalai Lama on his distinguished guests. It proves to be a happy housedog.

Below: The Tibetan terrier was the country dog of Tibet, but has adapted well to modern life in the normal household and has an appealing, mischievous nature.

LHASA APSO
Hardy, happy housedog; rather suspicious of strangers; good with children.
Color: All colors accepted.
Height: 10-11 in.
Coat type: Heavy, hard, straight, of good length; needs full brushing and combing every day.
Exercise: Needs quite a lot of exercise.

POODLE
Highly intelligent; good family dog; very good with children and with other pets; responds well to correct training.
Color: Clear colors preferred; coat should be an even and solid color at the skin. Blue, gray, silver, brown, café au lait, apricot and cream dogs show varying shades of the same color; brown and café-au-lait poodles have liver noses, eye rims, and lips, dark toe-nails and dark amber eyes. Black, blue, gray, silver, cream and white poodles have black noses, eye rims and lips, black or self-colored toe-nails and very dark eyes.
Height: Standard poodle – over 15 in; *miniature poodle* – 10-15 in; *toy poodle* – under 10 in.
Coat type: Naturally harsh, dense and curled; needs to be groomed daily with a wire pin comb or brush and bathed regularly; professional trimming or clipping into a suitable 'cut' is required.
Puppy Clip This clip is suitable for a poodle under one year old. The face, throat, feet and base of the tail are shaved; there is a pom-pom on the end of the tail.
English Saddle Clip Here the face, throat, feet, forelegs and base of the tail are shaved, leaving puffs on the forelegs and a pom-pom on the tail. The hindquarters are covered with a short blanket of hair. The body is left unclipped but may be shaped.
Continental Clip Here the face, throat, feet and base of the tail are shaved. The hindquarters and legs are shaved, leaving pom-poms on the hips, bracelets on the hindlegs and puffs on the forelegs. There is a pom-pom on the end of the tail.
Sporting Clip Here the face, feet, throat and base of the tail are shaved leaving a cap on the head and a pom-pom on the tail.
Exercise: Enjoys a moderate amount of exercise.

SCHIPPERKE
Good family dog; excellent guard dog; loves children; shy with strangers; very hardy.
Color: Solid black.
Weight: Up to 18 lb.
Coat type: Abundant and harsh to the touch; needs very little grooming.
Exercise: Very flexible; likes a good walk, but can manage without.

TIBETAN TERRIER
Happy and extroverted housedog; rather mischievous but responds to careful training; good with children.
Color: Any color including white.
Height: 14-16 in.
Weight: 22-23 lb.
Coat type: Long, fine and straight top coat, fine undercoat; needs very thorough brushing every day.
Exercise: Enjoys long walks, but can manage without.

Here a Standard Poodle overshadows his diminutive Toy Poodle cousin, though both have similar trims. Poodles are intelligent and very affectionate towards their owners.

The champions

Champion dogs can be elevated to this status at a dog show, where they are judged on conformation, or at obedience or field trials, where they are judged on ability. There are other ways of competing with dogs, too, which may not make them official winners, but will make them true champions in the eyes of their owners.

A West Highland White Terrier proudly poses with his cards, ribbons and impressive trophies won as best exhibit in an English dog show.

In 1884, a group of amateur sportsmen founded the American Kennel Club (AKC) in order to establish a set of uniform rules for the exhibition of pedigree dogs. A non-profit organization, the AKC maintains a registry of recognized dog breeds and authorizes more than 8000 shows annually, to be run under its rules. It also aims to foster and encourage interest in pure-bred dogs, and their health and welfare. The AKC is comprised of about 400 clubs, each of which elects a delegate to represent its members' wishes at the AKC, and from those delegates are elected the directors who manage the day-to-day running of the AKC.

Since its inception, more than 25 million dogs have been registered with the AKC and, at present, some one million names are added to the stud book each year. A monthly called *Pure-bred Dogs – American Kennel Gazette* is the official journal of the AKC and publishes news, views and reviews, gives official notice of all AKC events, decisions of the board of directors, and lists new champions and obedience degree winners, as well as printing interesting and well-illustrated articles. The AKC also publishes a monthly report of show, obedience and field trial awards; an impressive hardback book called *The Complete Dog Book;* various excellent information booklets and a series of color films complete with soundtracks, which may be hired by clubs.

The address of the American Kennel Club is 51 Madison Avenue, New York, NY 10010.

The American Kennel Club does not buy or sell dogs, neither does it grant a seal of approval to kennels whose names it accepts on to its register. Owners may register their kennel names with the AKC, protecting them for their sole use in registering dogs intended for showing and breeding. The AKC also maintains a register of individual dogs, and when purchasing a pure-bred dog you should ensure that the following points are covered:

1. A dog sold as being eligible for registration with the American Kennel Club should be supplied with an AKC application form, properly completed by the vendor; this is also filled by you as the purchaser, and sent to the AKC with the appropriate fee. After the details are processed you will receive an official AKC registration certificate.

2. AKC rules stipulate that a seller of dogs represented as eligible for AKC registration must maintain full identifying records, even though AKC records may not be available. The dog must be identified either by handing the buyer a properly completed AKC registration application, or a bill of sale, or a written and signed statement giving the following information: breed, sex and color of dog; date of birth of dog; registered names of the dog's sire and dam; name of the breeder.

3. It is the responsibility of the buyer to obtain sufficient information to allow AKC registration, but any purchaser encountering problems in buying dogs, or obtaining paperwork, should write with full particulars to the American Kennel Club.

Left: Showing his paces. An Old English Sheepdog runs out with his handler in order to show his straight, sound movement to the judge.

Right: Every breed has to be shown off in a certain way, with legs, head and tail held to enhance the dog's desired appearance. Handlers are adept at offering tidbits in such a way as to produce the correct stance and expression.

Dog shows

Of the 8000 or so canine events held each year under the rules of the American Kennel Club, the most numerous are dog shows, where the emphasis is placed on the dogs' conformation. Dog show judges examine the contestants, and assess them in accordance with the official standards for their respective breeds. There are two types of conformation dog show, the **all-breed** and the **specialty**. The first, as the name suggests, is for dogs for all breeds, while the specialty show is for dogs of a designated breed or group of breeds. Shows held under AKC rules are run by all-breed and specialty breed clubs. Each breed of dog recognized by the AKC has its national club, and some breeds also have local specialty clubs. The role of the clubs is of paramount importance to the AKC. Each club is responsible for the revision of breed standards and rules pertaining to a breed, and submits suggestions and formulations to the AKC for the approval of the board of directors.

Left: An exhibitor employs a portable grooming contraption to restrain her Komondor while she arranges its corded coat in order to impress the judges.

Below: The posterior view of a judging ring where Old English Sheepdogs line up for their final inspection before the placings are decided.

At the conformation dog show, judging is progressive, and works towards a climax which produces an overall best in show. Most of the dogs entered compete for points towards their championship; a dog needs fifteen points to become an official AKC champion and, essentially, an entrant gains points depending upon the number of other dogs it beats in competition. The points system is weighted according to breed, sex and the geographical location of the show. A dog can earn from one to five points at a show, and three, four or five points are termed 'majors'. To become a full champion a dog must gain its fifteen points under at least three different judges, and must include two majors won under two different judges.

Dogs competing for points at a conformation dog show are referred to as Class Dogs, and can enter for five regular classes as eligible: **puppy** – often divided into 6-9 months and 9-12 months; **novice; bred by exhibitor; American-bred; open.**

Dogs compete only against dogs, and bitches only against bitches, and judging is the same for every breed. First the judge takes the puppy dog class, and awards first, second, third and fourth; the winner remains in competition. Then the judge works through the rest of the classes and the five first-prize dogs are judged in the winners class to produce Winners Dog, the male which receives the most points at the show. The dog placed second to the Winners Dog in his original class is then brought into the ring and judged against the other class winners to produce Reserve Winners Dog. This award is made so that the Reserve may receive the points, should the Winners Dog be later disqualified for any reason. The same process is repeated with the bitches until a Winners Bitch and Reserve is selected. The judge then judges for Best of Breed from all the champions of record (in other words dogs already holding Champion status) that are competing, and the Winners Dog and Winners Bitch. Having selected one Best of Breed, the judge then selects a Best of Winners from the Winners Dog and Winners Bitch; if either the Winners Dog or Winners Bitch is Best of Breed, it automatically becomes Best of Winners. Finally the judge selects a Best of Opposite Sex to the Best of Breed winner. At an all-breed show, the same judging process continues through every breed; then every Best of Breed Winner competes for Best of Group. Four placings are given in each group, but only the first placings remain in competition.

Finally the six Best of Group winners are judged to produce the overall Best in Show exhibit.

Format for specialty and all-breed shows

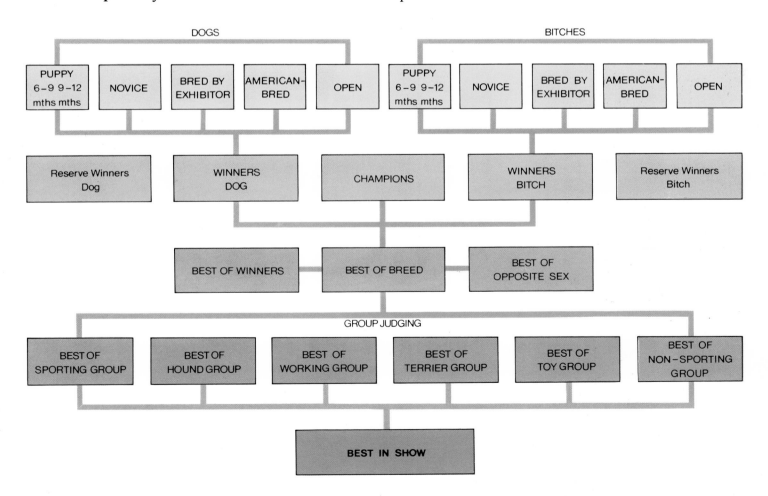

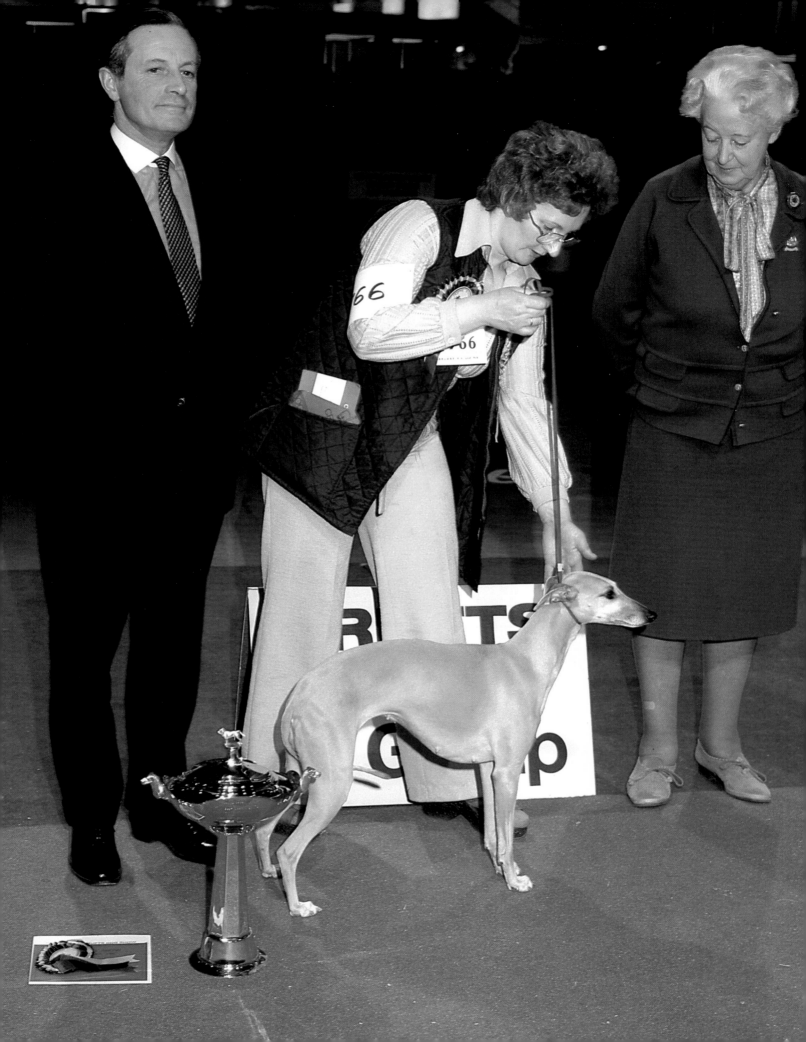

In contrast to the specialty or all-breed dog show is the dog match. This is conducted in a similar fashion to a dog show, but the dog match carries no championship points or obedience degrees. A match provides the ideal training ground for novice exhibitors and novice dogs alike. There is an air of fun and enjoyment, and the stress of competing for championships is removed. Winners usually receive trophies and ribbons. At a dog match, dogs may compete in obedience trials at various levels, or in conformation rings. Exhibitors gain valuable experience in ringcraft techniques and showmanship, and their dogs learn manners, and how to behave in front of the judges, the crowds and in close proximity to other dogs.

Junior showmanship

A club approved by the American Kennel Club to hold a licensed or members' all-breed or specialty show may also gain approval to offer Junior Showmanship competition at its show. The Junior Showmanship competition is judged solely on the skill and ability of the handler, and, although the dogs themselves are judged exactly as in a breed ring, the dog's conformation is not taken into consideration by the judge. Nevertheless, the dogs which take part must be eligible for dog shows or obedience trials.

The Junior Showmanship competition is divided by class and by age, and, occasionally, also by the sex of the handler. Exhibitors are aged from ten to sixteen years inclusive, and the classes are Novice (for those who have not won three first-place awards in Novice competition) and Open (for those who have achieved three first places in Novice competition).

Above: Junior Showmanship classes are devised to encourage early participation of young owners in the art of handling for exhibition. This girl takes pride in presenting her dog to its best advantage before the judge.

Left: At the world famous Cruft's Dog show in London, England, a Best of Group Winner is presented to the admiring audience.

Right: Golden Retrievers are tethered and protected from soiling their coats while they await their call to the ring at the Royal Canberra Show in Australia.

Obedience trials

In the obedience trial, each dog is called upon to perform a prescribed set of exercises, which are scored by the judge according to the rules of competition. Obedience trials test the skills of the handler and trainer, as well as the dog, and the animal's conformation has no bearing on the results.

Obedience is divided into three levels of progressive difficulty, and at each level the competitor aims for an American Kennel Club Obedience Degree or title.

LEVEL	TITLE
Novice	Companion Dog (CD)
Open	Companion Dog Excellent (CDX)
Utility	Utility Dog (UD)

In addition there are official tracking tests, which can result in a Tracking Dog (TD) title.

Novice trials test the basic exercises that dogs must master in order to be obedient and well-behaved companions. The six exercises which are tested are: heel on leash; stand for examination; heel free; recall; long sit; and long down. Open trials test seven exercises: heel free; drop on recall; retrieve on flat; retrieve over high jump; broad jump; long sit; and long down. Utility trials test: signal exercises; two scent discrimination tests; directed retrieve; directed jumping; and group examination.

Each dog must earn three 'legs' to achieve an obedience title, and for each 'leg' a dog must score 170 points out of a possible 200, and achieve at least 50 percent on each exercise.

Dogs which achieve the Utility Dog title can earn points towards an obedience trial championship. Championship points are earned by taking first or second place in either Open B or Utility class. The dog needs 100 points to become an obedience trial champion and it must have won a first place in utility competition with at least three dogs in contention, a first place in Open B competition with at least six dogs in contention, and a third first prize in either of these competitions. In addition, the three first places to be counted must have been awarded by three different judges.

Left: A Rottweiler is sent out to retrieve his dumb-bell . . .

Left: Training a dog for Obedience Trials takes many hours of patient and repetitive work. Some dogs, like this Border Collie, excel at the High Jump after building up their muscle and ability at lower obstacles.

Right: . . . he picks it up correctly by grasping the center bar in his jaws . . .

Left: . . . and returns it to his handler.

Field trials

Like obedience trials, field trials test the working team relationship of man and dog. Field trials also test the ability of specific breeds to carry out the functions for which they were originally developed. The four categories of field trials are based on the field characteristics of the breeds involved: hounds, pointing breeds, retrievers, and spaniels.

More than 1000 field trials are held in the United States each year and these are not confined by the American Kennel Club to affiliated societies. There are three types of field trials. A **member field trial** is one at which championship points may be awarded and is run by an AKC member club; a **licensed field trial** is one run by a non-AKC club, but licensed by the AKC. Championship points may be achieved at a licensed trial. **Informal field trials** without championship points awards may be run by AKC and non-AKC clubs. These need AKC approval to be termed sanction field trials.

Any person of good standing may be approved to judge at a field trial, but dogs running in licensed or member field trials must be registered with the AKC.

Hound trials are very popular. The hounds are run as braces on cottontail rabbits; as small packs on rabbits and hare; or as large packs on hare only. Hounds are entered in classes according to their height, and are marked according to their performance. The hounds gain points for the title of Field Champion depending on their placing – the points being multiples of the starters in the competition. Trials for Beagles are most popular, trials for Basset Hounds are also run, and to a lesser degree, there are also trials for Dachshunds.

Trials for pointing breeds are very popular and are organized by specialty clubs all over the United States for the following breeds: Brittany Spaniels, Pointers, German Shorthaired Pointers, German Wirehaired Pointers, English Setters, Gordon Setters, Irish Setters, Wirehaired Pointing Griffons, Viszlas and Weimaraners. Trials vary, but may contain puppy stakes for young dogs of 6-15 months; derby stakes for dogs of 6-24 months; open or all-age stakes for dogs of any age over 6 months, and limited stakes for dogs over 6 months of age which have not previously won at trials. There are also trials for dogs belonging to novice and amateur owners.

In pointing trials, the dogs must cover large tracts of land in their quest for game, and the judges and handlers frequently work on horseback. The birdfields may have specially placed game for the dogs to find and point, and dogs may be required to retrieve fallen game. The number of points awarded to the winners

depends on the number of starters in each trial, to a maximum of five points per trial. The winner's points count towards championship status. A dog winning ten points in three different trials becomes a Field Champion, though in some breeds, points must have been achieved also in specified stakes. The winning of ten points in amateur stakes achieves for a dog the title of Amateur Field Champion. In addition, each breed club runs a national championship stake each year for which the entrants must qualify in previous trials.

Trials for retrieving breeds are run as closely as possible to a normal day's shooting. These trials are open to the various retrieving breeds and to Irish Water Spaniels. The dogs are required to fetch fallen game, shot by the hunter, from both water and land, and points towards championships are gained in a similar way to other trials.

Spaniels, with the exception of the Brittany Spaniel, are termed 'flushing' breeds, and are expected to quarter the birdfields within gunshot range of the hunter, to flush out the bird into the air to allow a clean shot, then to retrieve the fallen bird and return it to the hunter's hand. Spaniel trials, being so specialized, are less popular than other types of field trial. Nevertheless, some 40 trials for flushing breeds are held in the United States each year and are well attended.

Left: In pointing trials, dogs cover large tracts of land searching out game. Here a Pointer has located its quarry and adopts its typical 'pointing' pose.

Above right: Field Trials dogs must be trained to go wherever their handler commands, and this agile Labrador Retriever readily jumps into deep water when told to do so.

Right: Retrievers are expected to retrieve fallen game and to return it to the hunter's hand. Dogs like this Labrador have soft mouths and do not mark the game they carry.

What the judge looks for

How height and length are measured

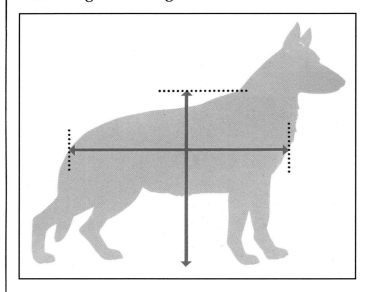

'A' Height – measured from a point horizontal with the highest point of the withers, straight down to the ground
'B' Length – from point of shoulder to point of rump

The dog's anatomy

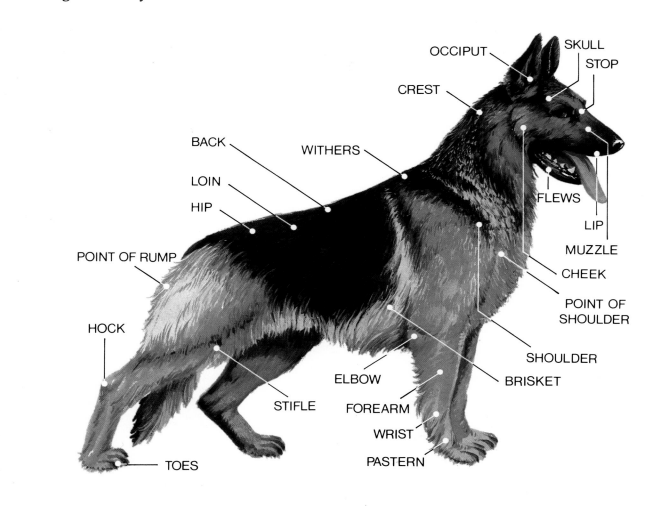

In each breed standard there is a section which describes specific disqualifying faults for that breed, but in addition there is a set list of disqualifying faults which apply to all breeds.

A dog which is blind, deaf, castrated, spayed, or which has been changed in appearance by artificial means, except as specified in the standard for its breed, or a male which does not have two normal testicles is disqualified. A male dog which has been castrated may be entered as a stud dog (judged on progeny), and a spayed bitch may be entered as a brood bitch (judged on progeny). The removal of dew-claws and the docking of the tail is not penalized if the dog is of a breed where such removal and docking is approved and not contrary to the breed standard. Spayed bitches and monorchid or cryptorchid dogs may compete in obedience trials.

A dog will also be disqualified if it appears lame (to be determined by the judge), or if it has been artificially prepared to alter the natural color or natural shade of color, patterns or marking, of if any cleaning or coat preparation substance remains in the coat.

Any dog whose ears have been cropped or cut in any way is prohibited from show entry in any state where the laws prohibit such cropping or cutting. Also disqualified is any dog showing clinical signs of distemper, infectious hepatitis, leptospirosis, or any other known communicable disease, or any dog which has been in contact with any communicable disease within 30 days of the show, or has been kenneled within 30 days of the show on premises on which there existed any communicable disease.

A coveted First Prize Ribbon and winner's ticket are presented to a magnificent Bloodhound, shown to perfection by his young handler.

Show preparation

Show preparation really begins when you first decide to buy your puppy. It is pointless to purchase a pet dog, then expect it to become a show or obedience champion. If you plan a canine show career, study the breeds and decide on the one which is best for your purposes. Then make extensive inquiries regarding the top show kennels, contact them, and finally decide on the puppy which has the most potential. Having purchased the puppy, you must rear it carefully to ensure that the conformation develops to its fullest, within the dog's genetic confines, and that it has good bone and dentition. Diet also has a bearing on temperament – certain additives and colorings can make some dogs excitable; some foods can make a dog sluggish. A well-balanced diet helps to produce a well-balanced dog with a good coat and happy personality. The young dog must be carefully trained in good manners and basic obedience, then in ringcraft; or, if it is to run in obedience or field trials, its specialist training must commence as soon as it is mentally ready and physically developed and fit to cope with its tasks.

The breeder of your puppy will probably be of much assistance to you in the planning stages of your dog's show career. You must make sure that your puppy is correctly registered with the American Kennel Club, and is transferred into your ownership. You must also ensure that your puppy's vaccination program is properly followed, and that you know exactly how to groom, trim and prepare your chosen breed for the ring. You can buy books on most breeds, explaining the specific care and attention needed, and joining a club can be very beneficial.

The American Kennel Club has several very helpful booklets and you can write for a current list to the address on page 76. The titles include:

Rules Applying to Registration and Dog Shows, Obedience Regulations, Registration and Field Trial Rules, Beagle Field Trial Rules, Basset Field Trial Rules, Regulations for Junior Showmanship, Match Regulations, Dogs: General Information.

You can find out about clubs, local dog shows, matches and trials from the canine specialist magazines, published monthly, and from advertisements in your newspaper. Perhaps the most important aspect to remember in preparing for a show, match or trial is that showmanship is an enjoyable hobby and, while it is most satisfying to produce a winning dog, win or lose, you will have an exciting and rewarding time and will make many new friends.

Left: Each breed has its own requirements in show preparation. This Afghan Hound has the long silky hair on its ears protected from immersion in its dish by covering them with a special knitted helmet.

Right: Last minute trimming before a trio of Sealyhams take their places in front of the judge.

Action dogs

Since the early days of its domestication the dog has proved to be the willing servant and loyal companion of man. Today's working dogs take part in sport, hunting and racing, they herd cattle and sheep, guide the blind, rescue climbers and hikers, haul sleds, and assist the police and the armed services in their duties.

The Labrador Retriever, an all-purpose breed which excels as a housedog and in working with the gun on land or in water – a true example of the action dog.

Scent hounds

Hounds that hunt by scent have deep muzzles and exceptional scenting powers – even if asked to follow an old, or cold, trail. Scent itself is very variable, and is affected by many factors including the type of terrain over which the quarry has passed, the climatic conditions and the quarry itself. The huntsman who controls the pack of scent hounds uses his voice or a hunting horn to relay signals and – depending on the hounds, their quarry and the location of the hunt – different calls are used to tell the hunt followers what is happening in the field.

There are many different types of scent hound, including foxhounds, harriers, beagles, bassets and bloodhounds. Some are hunted after live quarry, others on drag lines where an artificial trail is laid by a runner on foot or by someone crossing country on horseback. Hounds are laid on the trail and track down the quarry by following the scent, no matter how this twists, turns and meanders.

The most numerous of scent hounds is the foxhound, and in the United States the English and the American Foxhounds are popular, as are various cross-bred packs. As its name suggests, the foxhound is bred to hunt the fox; the first English Foxhounds were brought to the United States by Lord Fairfax in 1738, and today there are over 100 packs of foxhounds. The English Foxhound is sturdier than the American Foxhound, the latter having been developed from crosses between the English hounds and imports from France and Ireland. Today's foxhounds are used for four diverse purposes for which four different types of hound are required: the field trial hound must be fast and rather competitive in nature; the hound used for hunting a fox with a gun calls for a slow-trailing, methodical hound with a really good voice (in other words a voice that relays information back to the owner); the trail or drag hound which is raced or hunted on a drag line must be accurate and very fast, as speed alone produces a winner; and the pack hound must conform to pack life, and work methodically and well in a pack of around twenty or more foxhounds.

The Harrier, which is slightly slower and smaller than the foxhound, was developed for hunting the hare, and has been worked in the United States since colonial times. Today, this breed is popular for drag hunting, and the foot followers have been largely replaced by those on horseback.

The Beagle is also very popular, and is used to hunt

in a pack for hare or cottontail rabbit. The Beagle provides good sport and is also a favorite of huntsmen who want to keep a few hounds of their own to hunt individually.

Basset Hounds are used to hunt rabbits, though they have also been trained to hunt other game such as raccoons, and to trail, flush and retrieve game birds. Slow, and with a good voice, the Basset is renowned for its exceptional trailing qualities.

The Black and Tan Coonhound, as the name suggests, was developed to hunt raccoons, though it has shown considerable skill in hunting deer, mountain lion and bear. This hound trails entirely by scent, and gives voice when its quarry is treed or cornered. The breed was officially recognized in 1945.

Like the Coonhound, the Bloodhound works tirelessly on the scent trail. Developed to hunt fugitives, the Bloodhound tracks but does not attack its quarry. Today's Bloodhound is used in search and rescue work as well as by police trailing fugitives from the law, and some dogs of this breed have proved outstanding in obedience work.

Dachshunds, or badger-dogs, were used in their native Germany to hunt the badger – following it underground when necessary – and to tackle wild boar, foxes and wounded deer. Very few Dachshunds are hunted today, but the breed does feature in field trials.

Left: At the meet, in Hamilton, Massachusetts, the huntsman reinforces his relationship with his Foxhound pack.

Below: A pack of Foxhounds hot on the scent of their quarry streak across the meadow in pursuit of the elusive fox.

Sight hounds

Sight or 'gaze' hounds look quite different from scent hounds, being built for speed. The most numerous are the Greyhounds, which are popular on the track, and race after a mechanically operated dummy hare. Greyhounds probably came to America in the early sixteenth century, and were useful hunters. General George A. Custer was fond of the breed and kept several hounds which he used in matched races.

The Borzoi is a Russian breed, developed to hunt the wolf, but today it exists mainly as an aristocratic show dog, though its high intelligence and response to training has resulted in the winning of obedience certificates. The Irish Wolfhound is the tallest of all dogs and, like his Russian cousins, is no longer hunted but proves a winner in obedience competitions and coursing trials.

The Afghan Hound was the Royal Hunting Dog of Afghanistan. This ancient breed was first kept as a palace dog in the country of its birth, and used for coursing game for the falcon, and the gun, over difficult terrain. Today's Afghan Hound is a super show dog, though it has shown great talent in lure racing, and when carefully trained, has reached high standards in obedience work.

The Saluki is the oldest known breed of dog, and is depicted on Ancient Egyptian tombs dating from more than 2000 years ago. The dog was also mummified after death and many well-preserved examples have been discovered in their masters' tombs and in special dog cemeteries of the time. The Saluki is raced in the United Kingdom and continental Europe, and is also used for hare-coursing in the United States, but is basically a house and show dog.

The Scottish Deerhound is very like a Greyhound in conformation but has a rough coat, and is a rare dog with a very ancient history. The breed has excellent scenting powers as well as keen eyesight, and is extremely fast. Though originally developed to run down deer in the Highlands of Scotland, the Deerhound soon adapted to life in the United States, where the hunting of antlered game with dogs is prohibited, and became proficient at hunting wolves, coyotes and rabbits.

Below: Built for excessive turns of speed, Greyhounds become a blur on film as they race past the camera after the mechanical hare.

Right: The Scottish Deerhound is similar to the Greyhound in build but has a dense rough coat. Once bred for the hunting of Red Deer in Scotland, this rare dog is now kept as a prestigious pet.

Racing dogs

The sport of Greyhound racing evolved naturally from coursing, although it was many years before racing with dogs became really popular. It was reported in the English *Times* newspaper dated September 11, 1876 that a form of racing with Greyhounds took place behind an inn called the Welsh Harp. Several races were run over a track 400 yards long, along which a grooved runway had been laid to carry an artificial hare, which was pulled along in advance of the dogs by means of a windlass. The English coursing enthusiasts were very opposed to this new sport, and it was left to the Americans to devise and develop dog-racing in an organized manner.

From the year 1874, dogs were raced on horse-race tracks, then, in 1909, the first official Greyhound track opened with a grand meeting in Tucson, Arizona. Since those far off days, Greyhound racing has become very popular throughout North America, and in Britain, Australia, and many other countries of the world. In Spain, Greyhound racing now competes with bull-fighting as the country's most popular spectator sport, and with dogs imported from the United States, Britain and Ireland, the standard of competition is very high.

It is not necessary to be rich to own a racing Greyhound, though training and kenneling costs can be quite high. A suitable puppy must be purchased, and very carefully reared, being fed a special balanced diet and given exactly the right sort of exercise to develop its racing muscles. When it is old enough, the puppy is passed into the care of a licensed trainer and it learns manners and how to chase a mechanical hare.

Preliminary trials determine the young dog's potential, and when the trainer deems it the right time, the puppy will be entered for these trials.

Greyhounds race at seemingly breath-taking speeds over measured distances, which vary from sprints to staying races, and sometimes over hurdles. They may, in fact, reach average speeds of around 38 miles per hour. Commercial Greyhounds live quite pampered lives in kennels, being carefully fed and specially groomed to the peak of condition. A dog is in top racing condition for about three years, during which time it receives the best of attention. On race day, strict routines are observed as regards feeding and exercise, and the dog is carefully groomed to tone up the muscles. Once the dog arrives at the track it is tested for the presence of drugs and for fitness to run.

Thousands of Greyhounds are bred for the racing industry but only about 75 percent of the puppies are found to be of the correct temperament and conformation for racing. Discarded Greyhounds may be humanely destroyed, sold for research or passed to pet homes.

The Whippet is an English Greyhound in miniature and was originally called the 'snap-dog', being used for 'snap-dog coursing' in which the winner was the dog which snapped up the greatest numbers of rabbits during a match. Later, the Whippet became a racing dog over a standard course of 200 yards. Each dog has two attendants: a slipper and a handler. The slipper holds the dog on its handicap mark while the handler takes his place at the finish with a lure of a colored rag or towel to which the dog is trained to run. At the signal to go, the slipper hurls the dog into the race by its scruff and butt, and it races to the handler's lure. Whippets are very variable in size and weight and are handicapped accordingly. At some tracks, electric starting boxes are used, and steeplechases have also been inaugurated.

Left: Probably the fastest breed of dog over short distances, the Greyhounds here race around a turn in the track as they vie for the lead in an important race.

Right: Dog-racing is a popular sport in many countries of the world and breeds other than Greyhounds are sometimes entered into competition. Afghan Hounds show a good turn of speed and train well to the track.

All manner of dogs are used for herding the world over and small indigenous populations of dogs are developed for their talent for working in local conditions. This young puppy is taking his first lesson in watching the flock.

One of the oldest functions of the dog is that of herding man's flocks. Herding dogs are found throughout the world and show great variation in type, size, color and conformation. Though most herding dogs show a natural flair for the job, careful training is necessary to produce a dog's true talent. Formal training in shepherding starts at around six months of age with basic training including heeling and the sit command. The young dog is taught to accept the sheep long before it is expected to work with them, and a series of whistle commands or gestures is gradually introduced. Eventually the dog accepts all of its handler's commands and will stop, go to the left or right, lie down, come forward and run out to gather sheep, all from the minimum of gestures, whistles or verbal commands.

Dogs are used for droving cattle as well as herding sheep but, whatever the purpose, it is an inspiring sight to watch a well-trained herding dog or two hard at work, or in competition.

The best known of all the herding breeds is the German Shepherd or Alsatian, though it is rarely used for herding these days, having become more popular as a police dog, a rescue dog and an effective guard. The Border Collie is the most commonly used dog for herding sheep and in sheepdog trials. This dog has only recently joined the ranks of recognized breeds, due mainly to its lack of written pedigree records. The Border Collie, which is of variable type, is an excellent herder and also makes a fine obedience dog. In the past, the Rough or Scottish Collie was popular, and gained public support following the famous series of 'Lassie' films in which the star was a talented Rough Collie which performed amazing feats of bravery, intelligence and endurance.

The Sheltie looks very much like a miniature version of the Rough Collie. It is a true sheepdog from the Shetland Islands off the north coast of Scotland which, in its day, was an excellent herder of the island's wild and wiry sheep. Today's Old English Sheepdog rarely works, having been developed as a show dog. It has utilitarian roots, however, having been used as a drover's dog in England during the seventeenth and eighteenth centuries when it was known as the Bobtailed Collie. There are lots of shaggy-looking sheepdogs similar in type to the Old English scattered throughout the world where they carry out herding duties and guard their flocks against various predators. An example is the Briard or Chien Berger de Brie in France, and there are many others without the benefit of breed names.

Some countries have unusual herding breeds. There is the Huntaway of New Zealand, which keeps in touch with base by constantly barking while working high in the hills. Australia has the unique Kelpie, a small wiry sheepdog capable of working large herds on the open range, without any assistance. The Australian Heeler or Cattle Dog is also a good worker, driving cattle by nipping their heels. The Corgi breeds of Wales are heelers, too, though today they are more likely to grace the show ring than a cattle drive. In the fifteenth century, the Corgi was used to drive herds of Welsh black cattle eastwards to London. The dogs drove the cattle during the day, keeping them to the side of the narrow roads, and protected them from thieves at night. Following the sales, the dogs protected the drovers and their money as they began the long trek back to Wales, often at the mercy of thieves and footpads lying in wait along the way. The Swedish Valhund is very similar to the Corgi, and is primarily used for working cattle, though it is also useful with sheep.

Some sheepdogs, like the Komondor and Puli from Hungary, have remarkable coats of long hair which form into corded ropes, quite disguising their canine shape and allowing them to merge naturally with the sheep they guard so efficiently. The large white Komondor blends beautifully with the semi-wild native sheep of the prairies, while the smaller, dark-coated Puli merges with the flocks on the edge of the plains.

Ability has always been more important than looks in a working sheepdog, and a talented dog has always been in demand for breeding purposes. Because of this, local type has been permanently set over the generations, by the careful selection of the dogs and bitches allowed to breed.

Below: The trust in their protector felt by the lambs is apparent in this poignant picture of a shepherd with his flock and herding dog.

Gun dogs

Strangely enough, the history of today's gundogs far predates the invention of firearms, for dogs with similar tendencies were prized for centuries for their ability to find, flush and retrieve game hunted by other means.

In the seventeenth century when the 'fowling piece' first came into use, it brought new problems along with its greater accuracy and range of kill. The muzzle reload process was long and tedious, and if the game was flushed before the hunter was ready the shot was lost. The hunter soon realized the worth of setting and pointing dogs, specially bred and trained to find game, then to freeze, standing quite motionless while pointing out the game, until the hunter was ready to fire. Breach-loading weapons were developed next, and the spaniels became popular, being ideal for entering any type of cover to flush out game. Retrieving dogs were needed, too, for the quick collection of fallen game and its safe return to the hunter's hand.

Through the centuries, man and dog have worked closely together in all weathers and over all types of country, and each of the gundog groups has been developed to give us the beautiful and efficient breeds of today.

It is the dog's natural hunting instinct that makes a good gundog, though this instinct is suppressed to a certain degree, so that the dog does not pursue or catch its quarry, but rather waits for the hunter to dispatch it. This requires a considerable degree of control in the dog, and this has been bred in by careful selection over the years. The gundog hunts with enthusiasm tempered with restraint, and this is achieved only when the submissive instinct is balanced equally with the hunting instinct.

Gundogs are divided into various groups depending on the task they are expected to perform. Some flush out game for the gun, some point or set – indicating the whereabouts of the game – and others retrieve shot game.

In 1789, a book was published called *An Essay on Shooting*, which describes three types of dogs capable of being trained by the hunter. These were the Smooth Pointer, the spaniel and the Rough Pointer. A later book, *Encyclopedia of Rural Sports*, published in 1840, informs us that the spaniel group includes the setter, the 'Common Spaniel', the Newfoundland Dog and the retriever. Spaniels have the longest history of any gundog, and were first used in Spain to drive ground-dwelling birds into waiting nets. The spaniel became a fashionable dog in the seventeenth century. Henry II of France was fond of them and the marriage of Charles I of England to Henrietta Maria of France brought the breed into favor in England. Easy to train and economical to keep, the spaniel has continued to be valued through the ages. The use of the spaniel in flushing woodcock gave it the name of Cocking Spaniel or Cocker, while other spaniels became adept

at startling game, and so were called Starters or Springers. The American Cocker originated in America in the 1870s, being bred from the English Cocker and the American Brown Water Spaniel, a dog famous for its work in marshlands.

In the mid seventeenth century the pointer was used to find and flush hares for its working partner, the Greyhound, to chase and kill. Spanish Pointers were crossed with foxhounds to produce the true pointer which has remained of similar type to the present day. The German Shorthaired Pointer came from similar rootstock, with some Bloodhound added to improve its scenting powers, and some foxhound to give added stamina.

The Magyar or Hungarian Vizsla is the national dog of Hungary, and is similar to the German pointing breeds. A dog with the Vizsla's characteristics is featured in a fourteenth century manuscript, showing its use in falconry. Eventually the breed was selected for its unique russet-gold coat. It is an efficient and attractive gundog. Another unusually colored gundog is the Weimaraner, often called the 'gray ghost' because of its light mouse-gray coat. The Weimar Pointer, as it was first known, was originally bred for hunting big game including wolves, lynx, deer and bear. Eventually, a breeding pair was bought by Howard Knight, who took them home with him to the United States, where they caused a sensation, and became a popular breed of bird-dog.

Left: A trio of English Setters quarter for game, following traditions developed over the centuries.

Above right: A soft-mouthed Labrador Retriever returning a pheasant to the gun negotiates a snow-clad stone wall on his run in with the bird.

Right: Working as a pair, two Weimaraners stand motionless, pointing the game for the hunter.

Setters were mentioned in several early books on hunting, particularly black and tan setters, probably the forebears of the Gordon Setters kept in large numbers by the fourth Duke of Richmond and Gordon, in Scotland. The 'Setting Spanyel' of 500 years ago was far removed from today's English Setter, although it was almost certainly its ancestor, but by the sixteenth century two quite distinct types of bird-dog had evolved, the setting dog and the spaniel. In Ireland, the long-legged spaniel was favored, and this in turn probably produced the Irish Setter, which was either red or red and white. Until the year 1850, pointers and setters were both expected to perform as dual-purpose dogs: finding, setting and pointing, then retrieving game. Later it was decided to develop specialized breeds for retrieving. Setters, pointers and the larger spaniels were used as foundation stock, and crossed with Newfoundlands and other breeds. In a classic work published in 1847 called *Dog Breaking*, there is a good account of the retrievers' history: 'the best land retrievers are bred from a cross between the setter and the Newfoundland or the strong spaniel and the Newfoundland, not the heavy Labrador, but the far slighter dog reared by the settlers on the coast, a dog that is as fond of water as of land.' This breed became known as the Labrador Retriever, a fine dependable gundog, guide dog and police dog. Labrador Retrievers crossed with setters of the Gordon and Irish strains produced Wavy-coated

Retrievers, and selective breeding from this stock produced the Flat-coated Retrievers. For water-fowling, a dog with a special coat was needed, and crosses were made with the Irish Water Spaniel to produce the solid black or liver colored Curly-coated Retriever.

In 1807 an English brigantine foundered off the coast of Maryland, and among the survivors rescued by the American ship *Canton* were a pair of puppies, one red and one black; these were to found the breed of gundog known as the Chesapeake Bay Retriever which excels in water, especially at retrieving duck.

The Golden Retriever is as popular as a family pet as a gundog, and excels in both spheres. It has much mystery attached to its ancestry, one legend suggesting it was once a circus dog, another that a golden colored 'sport' was born in a litter of black retrievers, and was given away. It is certain, however, that the breed was known in Scotland and properly recorded from the year 1835, and that a small Water Spaniel and a lightly built Newfoundland were used in its development, with later crosses back to other Water Spaniels and to Irish Setters. The breed standardized and became renowned for its work on land and in the water, and for its glorious color. The Golden Retriever came to the United States in the 1890s but was not registered until 1925. Today the breed is popular for field trials, hunting and obedience work, as well as being the perfect guide dog for the blind.

Left: Perhaps the most dependable of the retrievers is the Labrador, bred from a cross between the Newfoundland and setters or spaniels, and then refined.

Right: An English Setter at work among the heather in the hill country of Scotland.

A member of a Husky team shows submissive behavior to the leader before the start of the day's work in the traces.

The two main categories of dogs used for hauling are the Spitz varieties, which developed in cold climates, and the stockier mastiff types found in warmer areas. Of the two types the Spitz group is better known, and the most famous members of the group are the Eskimo dog or Husky, the Alaskan Malamute and the Siberian Husky. These dogs have been used for generations for hauling heavy sleds, and without them many human settlements in remote regions would have been impossible.

Sled-dogs were recorded in a fourteenth century account of travel in Mongolia, and the dogs have remained virtually unchanged in type since those days. The best sled-dogs are short and square, with powerful chest muscles enabling them to pull heavy loads over long distances. The Siberian Husky is considered superior in pulling power and stamina and, like all sled-dogs, seems able to thrive and work on a diet that would be turned down by most dogs. Despite having a reputation for being short-tempered, Huskies of all types respond well to training and develop a strict pack order within their team, which must be understood and respected by their handler. In some cultures, the sled-dogs are kept for hauling for four to five years, then they are killed for their meat and hides, the hides being made into linings for coats, boots and mittens. As each dog reaches the end of its hauling life it is replaced by a younger, stronger dog, and the relative positions of the dogs in the team are changed until a new working balance is achieved.

In northern Canada sled teams are used to carry urgent mail and supplies to remote areas, and the Royal Canadian Mounted Police used superb teams of well-trained Huskies in their work in patrolling the Northwest Territories.

At the turn of this century, during the Great Gold Rush days, miners spent their spare time drinking and racing their dog teams against one another. In 1907, the Nome Kennel Club was formed and a course covering over 400 miles was devised for sled teams to negotiate, with a prize of $10,000 for the winner. Most of the teams taking part in the race were large Malamutes, but a Russian trader imported a team of Siberian Huskies, which, despite their smaller size, soon proved their bravery and endurance by coming in a close third overall, from a large entry in the 1908 race. In following years, the Siberian Husky teams have regularly given good performances and their popularity has increased.

In 1925, Nome, Alaska, was hit by a diphtheria epidemic, and dog teams were harnessed to carry the vital life-saving serum from Anchorage to the stricken town, a distance of 658 miles. The weather was appalling, with an 80 mile per hour blizzard, as the dogs put their shoulders into their harness and set off. It was to take five days for the serum to arrive, and, as the time ran out, Nome's top team-driver set out to try to intercept the incoming team. The driver, Leonnard Seppala, and his Siberian Huskies traveled 80 miles on

To celebrate the first emergency sled trek to Nome, Alaska, in 1925, an annual race called the Iditarod is staged. Here a competing team prepare for the start.

the first day, with temperatures 30°F below zero. The next day, when he had virtually given up hope of finding them, he met the incoming team at the point of exhaustion, and collected the vital serum, racing with it back to Nome. Today, intrepid teams and their drivers undertake the hazardous race to Nome in what has become a world-famous annual event to test the courage and endurance of men and women and their dog teams.

Guard dogs

Dogs have been used as guardians of the home for centuries, and special crosses were made to produce dogs for guarding duties. The early Mastiff was a formidable guard, but too slow to be relied upon to catch intruders, and the tough Bulldog was perhaps too aggressive, and too small. The gamekeepers of the large estates needed a special sort of dog to guard against poachers and personal attack, and so they tried crossing the Mastiff and the Bulldog and, happily, the perfect solution emerged in the shape of the Bullmastiff, a perfect guard. Great rivalry arose between the keepers, and various types of Bullmastiff were produced, all known as the Gamekeepers' Night Dog, renowned for their fearlessness and ability. Contests were held to test the Night Dogs' ability, the dogs being muzzled and slipped after a man was given a good start. The dog chased the man and knocked him to the ground, holding him securely for his keeper. In some contests the man was armed with a stout club, but in many years of such events no man ever held his own against a muzzled Night Dog.

The Bullmastiff is a model guard dog, good-natured and easily trained, totally fearless and completely protective of its environment and family. A good guard dog should deter intruders by its appearance alone, and should be able to give a good account of itself if attacked. It should not bark incessantly at every noise, but should be able to differentiate between voices, footfalls and car engines, giving a warning only when a stranger approaches or a strange car drives in. A nervous dog is useless as a guard and may bite its owners when under stress. A good guard, properly trained, will not only protect, but will also drop its guard at a command from its owner.

Security dogs are trained to respond to several handlers and are carefully taught in all the basic obedience movements before starting their advanced program. Once they have proved their ability and work well on and off the leash, they are tested for fitness, and any dogs showing nervous symptoms or flaws in temperament are discarded. Advance training in security work includes climbing high fences and walls, crawling under and through obstacles and jumping through flames.

Many breeds make good family guards but, generally speaking, small breeds which bark at strange noises are better termed watchdogs, being too small physically to deter intruders. Some large dogs, particularly those of some gundog breeds, are hopeless as guards, liking all mankind, whether they know them or not. Most of the herding and droving breeds have a natural built-in protectiveness which makes them ideal guards, and some are particularly protective towards women and children.

The family guard dog must be carefully reared and trained. It must never, ever, be teased by any member of the family. It should have its own special place for sleeping and should be taught the perimeter of the territory it is expected to guard. The family guard dog should not be handled, played with, or fed by anyone outside its own family circle. The guard dog must not have or desire any relationship outside its own family.

Left: German Shepherd guard dogs on duty safely confined behind their wire mesh fence. This breed excels in guarding property against vandalism and felony.

Right: A German Shepherd dog being trained to protect property.

Inset: The Great Dane is a gentle giant in reality, but in effect his sheer size and bulk acts as an effective deterrent against intruders.

Police dogs

Dogs are used by the police forces of many countries of the world, and perform valuable work particularly in crowd control and in the capturing and detention of criminals. The most popular police dog is the German Shepherd or Alsatian, a breed which is valued for its qualities of fearlessness and trainability. Other breeds which have proved their worth in police work include the Rottweiler, the Dobermann Pinscher and the Weimaraner. For work where extra scenting powers are required the Labrador Retriever has proved perfect for detecting the presence of drugs or explosives.

The first dogs used by the police were Bloodhounds, and in England during the early part of the nineteenth century a Bloodhound was specially trained to detect sheep stealers. This dog gave demonstrations of its skills in tracking, even in the worst weather conditions, and probably acted as a good deterrent in its area. The first arrest of a man by a Bloodhound was recorded in the English New Forest in 1810. Some of the police Bloodhounds of the United States have exceeded top detectives in the number of arrests achieved; one dog alone being credited with more than 600 'collars'. A Bloodhound called Nick Carter was put on a trail that was known to be more than four days old, and followed it to the fugitive's arrest. This four-day record was set in the early 1900s, but has since been more than doubled, and today handlers from the National Police Bloodhound Association, along with search and rescue clubs, use Bloodhounds in their traditional role of following stale trails over formidable distances, usually with great success.

For police work a dog needs a sound constitution and good eyesight, keen hearing and exceptional scenting powers. It must be highly intelligent, with an equable temperament, and be bold but not aggressive. The dog also needs to look impressive, with an appearance of controlled power. Dogs taken by the police are given a thorough screening for soundness of physique and temperament before training is undertaken. Great attention is also paid to matching the dog and its handler, for the pair will work together for several years.

The initial steps in training concentrate on obedience work, first on the leash, then free. The dog learns to obey voice and hand signals, and work close and at a distance. When the dog masters the preliminary commands, it progresses to both high and long-jumping and its fitness is gradually developed. All the exercises are taught in a slow and methodical manner until each is thoroughly mastered, and a dog is never over-stretched at anytime in the training program. The advanced basic training includes tracking, in which a dog follows a complex combination of scent traces indicating one particular human being. The dog's brain analyzes the signals from its olfactory organs, allowing the discrimination of scents which make the odor of one human as individual as his fingerprints.

Police dogs are trained to attack only on the command of their handler, and then to bite and hold the fugitive's forearm. Some dogs are taught to attack under gunfire, and how to avoid being clubbed with a weapon. Despite their efficiency in an attack situation, police dogs are generally gentle by nature and totally reliable.

Left: For police work dogs are meticulously trained, not only in tracking, chasing and seizing fugitives, but also in fitness exercises which build their stamina and agility. Here a German Shepherd shows its prowess in the long jump.

Right: This black Labrador Retriever is a superbly efficient drug detection dog, used at major airports to seek and find concealed caches of drugs in passengers' luggage.

Drug-sniffing dogs

Dogs of the retrieving breeds, like the Labrador Retriever, are valued by the police for their exceptional scenting abilities in searching out concealed drugs and other substances. Such dogs are employed by police in several countries, patrolling at customs points at ports and airports. Each drug dog is trained to detect one particular substance, and becomes so proficient at its job that it can indicate the presence of that substance to its handler even in the most difficult of conditions, such as at a luggage carousel in a crowded airport reception area, when the substance is meticulously sealed and wrapped and in the center of a suitcase full of clothing.

Other dogs are trained to detect explosive materials, and these police dogs are also used at ports and airports, as well as being employed to check conference rooms and convention centers prior to the visits of politicians or dignitaries. This ability is naturally invaluable to man.

Security and prison dogs

The prison dog is really a guard dog in reverse, being employed to keep prisoners in rather than to keep people out. The first prison dogs were chosen for their fierce natures and biting ability but, eventually, police methods of selection and training were incorporated, with each dog being trained and handled by his own officer. Several breeds have been used in security work around the world. The German Shepherd was the first choice in many instances, and the Dobermann Pinscher was found to be a perfect deterrent on appearance and reputation alone. In more recent times, however, the Rottweiler has gained popularity for this exacting work and has more than lived up to expectations.

The Rottweiler is a very old breed descended from Mastiffs of the Middle Ages, then used for hunting wild boar. As hunting decreased, the dogs were developed as drovers' dogs, moving the cattle to market, and carrying home the drovers' money in pouches attached to their collars to prevent theft. In Germany, the breed developed as the Rottweiler Metzgerhund – the Butchers' Dog of Rottweil – a sturdy black and tan dog of good proportion, with great stamina and a strong protective instinct. It was first imported into the United States in 1931.

Dogs of the armed services

Dogs have always been used in warfare, the earliest records being on the bas-reliefs of almost 4000 years ago showing the armies of Hammurabi, King of Babylon, marching into battle accompanied by their Mastiff-like dogs of war. In modern warfare, many different breeds of dog have proved their worth, though unlike the ancient war dogs, they were not expected to fight. The German armies first realized the potential of war dogs and, from 1870, formulated breeding and training programs, encouraging small town dog clubs and inter-town matches to find the finest and best-trained dogs. By the onset of the First World War, the German nation had more than 6000 fully trained war dogs, which are said to have saved the lives of more than 4000 German soldiers who would otherwise have been killed or made prisoners of war.

The British lagged far behind, having started their training of war dogs in 1910. When the United States joined the war, an appeal for suitable dogs was quickly answered, and instructors were sent from Britain to America and to France to train thousands of suitable dogs. By the outbreak of the Second World War, the Germans had more than 40 000 proficient war dogs, and sent half of this force to Japan just prior to the devastating Japanese attack on Pearl Harbor in 1941. In 1939 the British made a national appeal for suitable dogs and trainers to work with the army and air force and the Government Guard Dog School was established, sending a team to set up a dog school in Belgium in 1940. War dogs proved their worth time and time again over the following war-torn years in Europe, and several breeds earned their medals, including Airedale Terriers and Boxers, which carried messages and medical supplies through shell-fire and across mine-fields.

Left: In Britain's Prison Service, German Shepherd dogs are used as guards to keep offenders in and others out of the maximum security areas. Each highly trained animal has its own handler with whom it spends its working life.

Right: A well-trained police dog with his handler guards Westminster Bridge, London, England.

Inset: In the armed services of the world, German Shepherd dogs are favored as messengers, guards and dogs of war. Training programs are extensive and planned to the range of the dog's natural fitness and agility.

WESTMINSTER
BRIDGE

Some old prints and drawings depict dogs leading their blind masters along by a chain or leash, but it is only in comparatively recent times that dogs have been specifically trained for this purpose.

In 1819 a book was published by Johann Lein, founder of the Institute for the Blind in Vienna, in which he set out basic principles for training dogs to lead blind persons. This book was obviously too advanced for its time, for nothing further was attempted in this field of study for another hundred years. It was in 1916 that a doctor walking in the grounds of a hospital accompanied by a wounded and blinded soldier received an urgent message. He left his German Shepherd guard dog with the patient and hurried away. Just then it started to rain heavily, and the doctor returned to find that his dog had led the sightless man back to the shelter of the building. The doctor was impressed by the dog's behavior and started a special school for the training of dogs to guide the vast numbers of casualties blinded during the First World War.

By 1925 the school had been adopted by the German Red Cross and news of its success was spreading around the world. Meanwhile, an American, Mrs. Harrison Eustis, founded a training establishment in Switzerland during the 1920s. She called it the Fortunate Fields Kennels, and used it for breeding and training German Shepherd dogs for use by the Swiss and Italian police forces, for work at customs points and with the army. Mrs. Eustis heard of the German work in training dogs to guide the blind. She visited the center at Potsdam, and wrote an enthusiastic report for *The Saturday Evening Post* in America.

Following the article, Mrs. Eustis received numerous letters including one from Morris Frank, a young blind American, asking her for help in obtaining a dog to guide him. Mrs. Eustis arranged for one of her best trainers to attend the Potsdam center and, on his return, set up a school for the training of instructors and dogs, and for the instruction of blind people to work with the dogs. The school was christened *L'Oeil qui Voit* or The Seeing Eye. Mr. Humphrey, the trainer, personally selected and trained a dog called 'Buddy' for Morris Frank, who in 1928 became the first American to own a guide dog. He wrote a book about his cherished bitch and called it *The First Lady of the Seeing Eye*.

Mrs. Eustis worked and traveled tirelessly in her work, lecturing and writing articles, and eventually she met Muriel Crooke, an English breeder of German Shepherd dogs. This meeting proved the starting point of a successful campaign to launch the training of guide dogs in Britain. From these beginnings have developed the various associations for training guide dogs situated around the world, which give a new meaning to life for so many blind people. Those who are fortunate enough to have seeing-eye dogs confirm that the animals benefit them psychologically as well as giving them increased mobility. The presence of the dog often encourages people to stop and talk to the blind person, and the owner is compelled to take more exercise than he would otherwise do, for the benefit of the dog. It takes about a year for the blind person and the dog to develop a perfect partnership, and in this time the owner becomes skilled in dog care, while the dog learns regular routes and its owner's habits. Many pairs form extremely close bonds and seem to develop almost telepathic contact with one another.

Left: The Seeing-eye dog is trained to wear this special harness which fits around the chest and is connected to the blind owner's hand by means of a semi-rigid handle.

Right: With the dog's harness correctly fitted and the handle held safely in the left hand, the blind person is able to walk with confidence across a busy road junction.

Young dogs for use in training programs to produce guide dogs for blind people are generally raised in normal family situations, where they learn the rudiments of obedience and to live in harmony with people and other pets. The dog learns all about normal household routines, becomes clean and tidy in its habits, and accepts normal discipline. Most seeing-eye dogs are in fact bitches as these are generally less aggressive than male dogs, and are less likely to be distracted by smells and other dogs. All guide dogs are spayed or castrated before their training commences. Most guide dogs are trained at special centers by highly experienced sighted handlers.

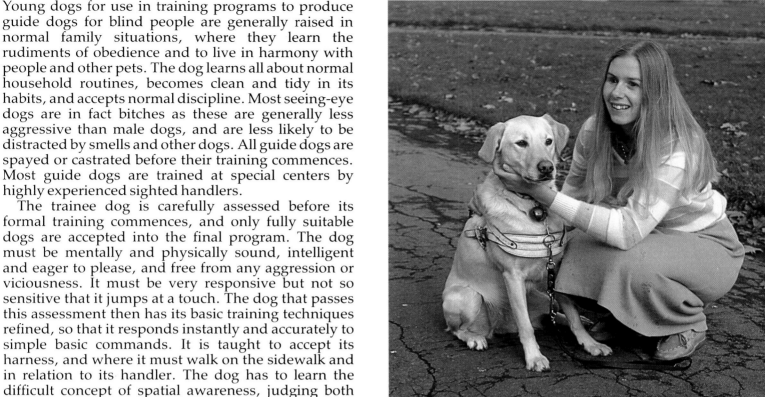

The trainee dog is carefully assessed before its formal training commences, and only fully suitable dogs are accepted into the final program. The dog must be mentally and physically sound, intelligent and eager to please, and free from any aggression or viciousness. It must be very responsive but not so sensitive that it jumps at a touch. The dog that passes this assessment then has its basic training techniques refined, so that it responds instantly and accurately to simple basic commands. It is taught to accept its harness, and where it must walk on the sidewalk and in relation to its handler. The dog has to learn the difficult concept of spatial awareness, judging both the height and width of objects to be negotiated, and it must learn the properties of traffic, near and approaching. These lessons are difficult to teach to the dog and often take some time before they are mastered.

The dogs are not worked for long hours in their harness and are given as much free-running time as possible each day, when they may romp and play in a relaxed manner. The seeing-eye dog soon learns that when its special harness is fitted on it means that work is about to commence, and when the harness is removed it means that the main responsibilities of its job are over for the time being and it is on 'free time'. The seeing-eye dog differs from all other trained dogs in that it is willing and able to override a command when it knows better than its owner. It might be told to move forward, but is aware of the approach of a fast-moving vehicle and so will refuse to move. This 'disobedience factor' can prove to be a life-saving device, and is one of the most important aspects of the dog's training.

Above right: A young blind girl comes to the end of her training program designed to acclimatize her to caring for and living with her very own trained guide dog.

Below right: A blind handler learns to fit his guide dog's special harness during the intensive training sessions designed to ensure that blind owners and their dogs are truly compatible and understand one another's signs and language.

Left: Great skill is required to train a dog to know when to overrule its master's commands, as here at a road crossing.

Historically, the most famous of all rescue breeds is the massive Saint Bernard, the ancestors of which are said to be the mighty Mollossian dogs of the Roman armies. One of the passes made by the Romans 2000 years ago was in the valley of Aosta, and was called the *Summum Penninus*. It formed an important route through the mountains of Italy to the north, and here the Romans raised a temple to Jupiter. Eventually, in AD 962, Bernard de Menthon came to the pass and built an Augustinian monastery, originally named in honor of Saint Nicholas, then renamed after its founder's death as the Hospice of the Great Saint Bernard.

The first mountain rescue dogs were trained at the monastery in 1665. They were selected from various alpine Mastiff types for their characteristics of strength, hardiness and obedience, and for a very special type of short dense coat, ideal for working in snow. The first dogs were of varied conformation but, as the generations passed, selection produced a definite type, first called the Alpine Dog, then the Alpine Mastiff, then the Hospice Dog and, finally, in 1880, christened the Saint Bernard. It has been estimated that in the past 300 years or so the Hospice Dogs have been responsible for saving the lives of more than 2000 people. 'Barry', the most famous of the dogs, has been credited with saving 40 travelers. Tragically, he was killed by his 41st casualty, who imagined him to be a marauding wolf.

The hospice monks used their trained dogs to search for travelers lost after snowstorms and avalanches, and it became a general routine to send out a pair of dogs to patrol about ten miles to the north of the hospice, and another pair to patrol up to ten miles to the south, at any time following a storm or severe weather. The dogs were trained to make their way to a rest hut, then to return to the hospice, and if they met anyone on the way, would try to induce the person to follow them back to the hospice. Only dogs were kept at the hospice, the bitches and puppies being housed at the monastery at Martigny.

The hospice is now run as an hotel, and rescues are carried out by vehicles but, in other remote regions of the world, mountain rescues are still carried out by descendants of the famous alpine dogs. In recent years, there has been a dramatic increase in the number of dogs used in mountain rescue work and most countries with high and inaccessible mountain ranges have their own efficient and well-equipped teams. Collies, Labradors and German Shepherds have proved excellent at such work, and the dogs often belong to volunteer rescue workers who have trained hard with their dogs to reach the necessary standards of proficiency. When they are accepted for training, the owner and his dog receive instruction and exercises similar to those given in police work. An intensive course in 'nose work' follows until the dog is able to locate a person buried under ten feet of snow, and dogs are expected to work as efficiently in darkness as in daylight. A probationary period is undertaken before the dogs are finally accepted on to the working team.

Both human and canine members of the teams exercise regularly, insuring that their efficiency is maintained at a very high level. Dogs are taught to accept transportation to inaccessible areas, and to accept the fitting of special harnesses which enable them to be winched down to mountain ledges, or to be lowered by rope from helicopters. Dogs have saved many lives by their swift and accurate location of persons buried under the snow, coupled with their relaying of the information by barking and frantic digging at the snow.

Left: In high mountain regions of the world, fully trained teams of rescue personnel and their dogs, mainly German Shepherds, wait for calls to action from parties trapped or stranded in inaccessible areas. Dogs are dropped by helicopter to seek and find mountaineers, and are later air-lifted out to safety.

Right: For over 300 years, Saint Bernard dogs have been trained and used for rescue work in the Swiss Alps. Descended from the Alpine Mastiff, the Saint Bernard is a strong dog and one of the heaviest of all breeds.

Training and obedience

It is possible to train any breed of dog, and the young mongrel puppy may prove as responsive to training as the most expensive of pedigree pups. Some individual dogs, and some puppies of specific breeds or selected bloodlines, tend to train more easily than others, but it is not always the most intelligent dog that responds most favorably to human commands. Some highly intelligent individuals resent each newly introduced exercise, regarding it with disdain and suspicion, and they have to be cajoled and coaxed into the right response. Such dogs have to be convinced that there is some point in the exercise, and even after learning the response will perform the exercise with a certain air of reluctance.

Some dogs have the aptitude to achieve exceptionally high standards in obedience work, and appear to enjoy every moment of training and exhibitions. Owners of shy or nervous dogs must be content with the performance of a few very simple, basic exercises. A dog's temperament is all-important when deciding on the form and extent of its training program, and the best type of dog for training is one with an even temper, a kind nature, and a bold fearless outlook on life in general. An introverted dog, perhaps badly reared, ill-treated, neglected or ignored as a puppy, may still be integrated into family life and may be trained in basic obedience if given plenty of time, patience and love, however.

The Basset Hound is amenable to training as long as there is a tangible reward at the end, and will happily 'Sit up' for a tidbit.

Choosing the right puppy

It is very important to examine your reasons for wanting a dog, and then, having decided to go ahead and buy one, to insure that you select the right breed or type to fit in with your own lifestyle and personality. Think carefully about your preference for a pedigree or a mongrel, whether you would prefer a dog or a bitch, whether you want a young puppy or would rather give a home to an older dog, and whether it would be better to have two dogs instead of just one. When making these decisions remember that whatever you decide the dog will be totally dependent on you, and you should be prepared to accept that responsibility for your dog during its lifespan. Life expectancy for a dog averages around ten years. Toy breeds, and the giants like the Great Dane, often have very short lives and are old at eight, while the medium-sized breeds may live into the late teens. Good feeding and the correct fitness program for a breed will prolong a dog's life, while poor diet and obesity may shorten it.

Before finally shopping for a dog of your own, you should also think carefully about how and where you will house and exercise it. Decide just how much you can afford, not only for the initial purchase, but also for the dog's upkeep. Expenses will include food, a license, vaccinations and veterinary fees, collars and leashes, feeding and drinking bowls, grooming equipment, a bed, and possibly fees for boarding kennels and training classes. Insure that you have enough time available each day for regular feeding, grooming, exercise, training and play. Remember, too, that puppies may be destructive, and some household items may need replacement.

When picking a puppy from the litter it is wise to see both parents if this proves feasible. Here a Standard Poodle bitch is shown with her litter and the litter's sire.

Choosing the right dog

DOG TYPE	ADVANTAGES	DISADVANTAGES
Pedigree or mongrel	Eventual size, shape, coat type and temperament known	May be expensive to purchase; some breeds of extreme type may need specialist care to keep them in top condition
	Inexpensive purchase price	Difficult to assess eventual size, shape, coat type and temperament
Dog or bitch	No unwanted pregnancies	May fight; needs correct discipline
	Fits readily into family structure and hierachy. Easily trained	Will come into season twice a year unless spayed
Adult or puppy	No early training required	Set behavior patterns may be difficult to change, may show jealousy
	Can be integrated into family home and brought up to fit in with your lifestyle	May take a while to house-break; may be destructive during first year or so.
One dog or two	Easier to train	May be lonely if left for long periods
	Two bitches generally get along very well	Two dogs may fight if aggressive breeds or habitual fighters like the terriers; a dog and a bitch get along very well but must be separated when the bitch is in season to prevent unwanted pregnancies

Picking a puppy
Always buy from a breeder, and try to see the whole litter with their mother if you can. Choose the boldest and strongest-looking puppy that is available, making sure that you do not have a last-minute change of heart regarding your pet's sex. Never take a shy or under-sized puppy merely because you feel sorry for it, or because the breeder offers it at a reduced price – it could cost double in the long term, needing extra care, special feeding or veterinary treatment.

LOOK FOR	AVOID
Bright eyes	Dull or discharging eyes
Clean ears	Ears with dark wax or grit inside
Cool moist nose	Dry nose or discharging nostrils
Firm body with elastic skin which, when lifted, springs back into place	Pot-belly, ribs showing, prominent hip bones, skin which feels stiff when gently grasped and lifted
Clean skin and fur around the anus	Stained or smelly skin or fur around the anus
Clean skin on body	Bare patches or redness of skin on body
Sturdy, steady movement	Lameness or weakness of movement

In choosing a puppy for children it is preferable for them to make their own selection. The Border Terriers here are being assessed for their temperament.

Early learning

The young puppy is similar to a young child; curious, investigative, and ready to experiment with each situation as it presents itself. This natural behavior must be made acceptable to produce a well-adjusted pet.

All training should be aimed at gaining the puppy's confidence, rewarding it with praise whenever it performs acceptably and administering quick, sharp correction whenever it misbehaves. Most dogs respond satisfactorily to a reward which is merely a word of praise and a rub of the ears or chest, and to a correction which is a stern, reproving 'No'. Both praise and correction must be immediate, otherwise the puppy will not understand your action.

House-breaking

The first major lesson that a puppy must learn is that there is an acceptable time and place for relieving itself. House-breaking can be a simple task with some puppies, while with others it can prove a long, frustrating process. The puppy's built-in behavior patterns help with all aspects of training, and house-breaking is no exception. The puppy has very little control over its bodily functions until it is at least twelve weeks of age; nevertheless, it usually moves away from its bed before emptying itself. You will notice, too, that your puppy wakes from a deep sleep, starts to romp and play for five to ten minutes, then it will sniff the floor, circle backwards and defecate. It will then probably play for another fifteen to twenty minutes and then sleep, and this completes the cycle which is constantly repeated. A puppy generally defecates about five minutes after eating a main meal.

Knowing when to expect defecation is a help in successfully house-breaking your puppy, as you then know just when to place it on its special patch of paper or earth. A great deal of patience is necessary at this time and the puppy must be praised profusely whenever it performs well, but must not be heavily chastised for making a mistake. Puppies may be trained in two stages if necessary: they can first be taught to empty themselves on newspaper then, when this has been successfully learned, they are retrained to use the garden or yard. With very young puppies, or in really harsh weather, this may be the only practical method of house-breaking; however, it does make the overall training more complex, and direct house-breaking is far more preferable.

For direct house-breaking choose a suitable area of the garden or yard. It should be well drained and

Left: In housebreaking the young puppy, it must be shown exactly where you wish it to pass urine or feces, and this should be in a well-drained area, unsoiled by other dogs.

Right: A litter of Weimaraner puppies play with a large, safe bone which is good for their teeth and gums and will not shatter into dangerous fragments.

spread with sand, gravel or some other easily raked material. Urine will filter through, and the droppings, when dry, may be picked up and disposed of. Lift your puppy and put it on its patch every time you may be fairly sure of results. Choose a suitable euphemism, 'Hurry up', 'Be quick' or 'Be good', used in a brisk encouraging tone, and be lavish with praise whenever the puppy performs. Never punish your puppy at this stage for making mistakes, and never indulge in the barbaric practice of rubbing the puppy's nose into its puddle. A stern 'No' is enough punishment for any sensitive puppy, and sounds similar to a bitch's remonstrative growl. Another acceptable method of chastising a puppy is to take the loose skin at the scruff, and shake it, along with the growling 'No'. Constant attention is vital if you are to successfully house-break your puppy, and once the lessons are learned, your vigilance and care are well rewarded.

It is best to confine the young puppy in a pen whenever it has to be left unattended. The floor may be protected with layers of newspaper, and the puppy should be provided with a bed and a non-spill bowl of fresh drinking water plus some favorite toys.

Bladder control at night is slow to develop, so you should plan to rise early and to wake the puppy, carrying it to its patch. A puppy urinates as soon as it is fully awake, and in this way a routine is quickly established and reinforces your training. If your puppy constantly defecates during the night, try changing the feeding routine. Give the final meal much earlier, or rearrange the order of the alternate cereal/milk, biscuit/meat feeds. By a process of trial and error you will discover ways of regulating your own puppy's digestion.

Keep your puppy clean and wholesome; wipe his feet with kitchen paper. Wash soiled areas of the floor with hot soapy water, rinse, then wipe with a mild solution of household bleach. Strong-smelling disinfectants should be kept away from young puppies as they may contain toxic ingredients or substances which may damage the puppy's pads if the puppy comes into contact with the chemical on the floor.

A puppy must be taught how to behave in a human environment, where it is allowed to go in the home, and what it is allowed to do. This training must commence as soon as the puppy is introduced to the household, and you must start as you mean to go on, never relaxing, for every time you give a command which is ignored you have, in fact, taught the puppy to be disobedient. The time to begin training varies from breed to breed, but can be any time after about six weeks, providing the puppy proves attentive.

Your puppy should have its very own bed or box, and it is useful to teach it to go there on command. Point your finger at the bed and choose a constant command 'Go to your basket' or 'Get in your bed'. This should be firm, but with no hint of anger otherwise the puppy will feel as if it is being chastised. If necessary, lift the puppy and place it in the bed, repeating the command, then reward with praise. Last thing at night, make the reward a small biscuit or chew-stick. The puppy should treat its bed as a private retreat and must enjoy going to it when told to do so. This is a valuable lesson and may save a puppy from harm when the command is given as a distraction from danger.

Teach your puppy to stay out of armchairs and keep it out of your bedroom. Your puppy should not be allowed to sleep on your bed; it may be unhealthy for you and is certainly unhealthy for the puppy. Decide which rooms are available to your puppy, and teach it to stay out of the others. Be sure to shut your puppy away on its own for periods each day so that it does not resent being alone. Start with a short period when the puppy is tired, and settle it in its bed with toys and a treat. Gradually lengthen the periods of temporary isolation, and in this way you will avoid having a dog which whines and barks whenever it is left.

The puppy's name

Waste no time in giving your puppy a suitable name, and stick to this name for the rest of its life. A short one-syllable name is best, or a flowing two-syllable one like 'Billy' or 'Tansy'. It is important to insure that your puppy's name does not sound like any of the command words that will be used in more advanced training later on. This word list includes 'No', 'Sit', 'Stay', 'Come', 'Heel', 'Down', 'Wait' and 'Leave'.

Start by calling your puppy in a coaxing voice, clapping your hands together or slapping them palms down on the floor, imitating a dog's own 'invitation-to-play' behavior. If the puppy ignores you, wait until it has finished examining the distracting object then try again. Wait until the critical moment when the puppy seems most likely to come before you actually call it. By giving a command where there is little likelihood of its being obeyed you merely reinforce disobedience. Coming to call is one of the most important lessons a dog has to learn. Puppies of some naturally wilful breeds may prove difficult to train. If such a puppy ignores a call, try turning and walking away. This usually produces the desired response. As soon as your puppy comes when called, reward it lavishly and end the lesson. Repeat this lesson often, adding the word 'Come' after the puppy's name. Always praise, and never allow the puppy to get bored. Never call your puppy by name when it is necessary to admonish or punish. Its name should always be associated with pleasantness and praise.

Using the word 'No'

The word 'No' should be used firmly and sternly every time the puppy acts in an unacceptable manner. This is an important command which will be used throughout the dog's life and must be taught correctly from the outset. Never use 'No' if there is a chance that you will be disobeyed, and do not use it so often that there is a danger of the puppy becoming immune to the command. 'No' may be reinforced by a reprovingly raised index finger or by slapping your hand against your leg, or clapping the hands.

Young puppies naturally carry objects around in their mouths and this behavior may be encouraged as it leads naturally to the 'retrieve' training given in later weeks. Lots of lavish praise should be given for a good performance as this helps to compensate in some measure for the number of times the 'No' command has to be given. Puppies vary immensely in temperament, but most are content with praise consisting of a short word and a pat, while others need to be greatly fussed with and petted. Try to avoid giving tidbits as rewards.

Play with your puppy, taking up various roles to replace its missing pack-mates. Puppies enjoy mock battles when you must pretend to be another dog of the same age, and 'tag' when you must first chase your puppy and then allow it to turn and chase you. Playing builds up a unique relationship between you and your dog. You must never allow your puppy to get over-excited, however, or allow its playful bites and snaps to become too realistic. If this situation starts to develop, use the 'No' command, followed by praise and a tactile reward when the puppy relaxes.

Above right: You may decide to allow your puppy to rest in one particular armchair, and this can be given special washable slip covers or cushions, which are changed when soiled.

Right: A really fresh beef shank bone is perfect for the puppy to chew on. When it becomes soiled or stale, dispose of it and give a fresh one, or a rawhide chew bone.

Left: The juvenile dog often chews on everything in sight and must be prevented from destroying the furniture or precious plants in the garden. Decide on objects that the puppy may be allowed to chew, and scold when anything else is chosen.

Most dog owners are content to have a happy, healthy dog around the house, a dog which allows itself to be groomed, comes to call and walks on the leash without pulling. Others would like to expand their dog's behavior repertoire but are unsure how to go about it. A few people have problem dogs, those which cannot relate to other dogs, people or pets, which cannot tolerate veterinary treatment or which have bad habits in the home. For any dog owner with a problem dog, or an owner who wishes to learn more about dog training procedures, there are dog training classes and clubs advertised in the canine press.

It is usual to enrol dogs for training at about six months of age. Younger puppies may be enrolled and go along to observe, gaining experience of being in the presence of other dogs and absorbing the interesting atmosphere. The owner also gains many tips and confidence by this process, before serious lessons are undertaken. A puppy may bark or whine with excitement at its first introduction to the training class, but it soon learns to socialize and to behave acceptably.

Normal training classes teach you to train your own dog in basic obedience, using simple equipment.– a metal link training collar and a leather or webbing training leash, six feet in length and half to one inch in width. The preliminary lessons cover all the basic techniques and commands, designed to produce a well-behaved and civilized dog which acts acceptably in all normal situations and which may be controlled properly on or off the leash. The exercises taught are exactly the same as those required by the American Kennel Club for the title of Companion Dog (CD). More advanced classes follow basic training for those who wish to achieve higher standards in obedience work for competitions.

You must always remember that training classes are not really for your dog; they are there to teach *you* to train and control your dog. Each dog is different and, though the basic rules usually work, it is up to each owner and trainer to use the techniques and commands in their own special and unique way to get the best out of their own pet. Perhaps the greatest secret of success in all forms of dog training is to reinforce every lesson learned with daily routine sessions. You need only run through the routine for twenty minutes or so each day, trying again when you experience failures, and praising each exercise performed well. Most dogs love these sessions, treating them like favorite games and, if you always end on a high note when your dog performs an exercise particularly well, you will find that lesson well learned. Most so-called failures in basic obedience are really due to a complete lack of practice sessions between classes, where the wayward dog has not been given the opportunity of fixing the commands and responses as behavior patterns.

Right: In training classes, owners are taught to teach and control their dogs. This Labrador Retriever is being ordered to 'Leave' as a ball is rolled past, and the dog sits motionless while the training collar remains slack on its neck.

Left: The French Bulldog is ready to accept his correctly fitted training collar which must be threaded exactly as seen in this picture, so that it has the correct action in use.

'Come'

At the start of each training session, reinforce your puppy's response to its name, and its willingness to come towards you when called. Make sure the training collar is correctly fitted and attach the training leash. Walk briskly forward, allowing your dog to walk or trot freely ahead at the extent of the leash. Stop walking and simultaneously call your dog's name, following this with 'Come' in an inviting voice, taking a step backwards and gently pulling the leash towards you. The first few times you try this exercise you may have to give the leash a short sharp jerk to gain the dog's attention and to encourage it to follow you as you move back. Eventually however, your dog will consider this exercise the equivalent of a game and will bound towards you showing pleasure. Take in the slack leash and give lavish praise.

The release word

The next step in basic training is to decide on a special release word for your dog. This must be chosen carefully as it should not be changed once taught. The release word is used to tell your dog that it has been released from the position of the last command. For example, when you have told your dog to 'Sit', it should remain in a sitting position until you give the release word. Many owners fail to realize the importance of the release word, confusing it with 'Good dog' or 'Good boy', and the dog will release every time it is praised, which is incorrect, and in some circumstances could prove dangerous.

Trainers use a variety of release words, 'OK', 'Paid for', 'Free now', and so on, but whatever word is chosen it should be in no way similar to any other word of command used in the dog's training program. The release word is often taught in conjunction with a tactile release gesture – a tap with the toe or heel against the dog's side, a hand gesture or something similar – and the dog may eventually respond to either the word or the gesture, or to the combination. Take care to differentiate between praise words and the release word, and do not allow your dog to release when praised. This is best achieved by insuring that your tone of voice is low and soft for praising, and higher with some excitement for the release. If your dog is inclined to release when praised, bring it back to the original position, praise lavishly while main-

taining leash control, hold the position for a ten-second or so count, then release.

The release is the dog's 'at ease' command, when it may romp and play as it pleases. The dog must accept praise words in any training position, realize that it is doing well, and maintain the position. Eventually the release may be given at a distance with equal success. As with all lessons, keep release word training sessions short and, if your dog becomes tired or bored, abandon the lesson, ask for a response that has already been mastered, and finish the session on a good note. The next day, start the session with the simple command on which you finished the previous day, then try the abandoned lesson again; in most cases the dog will have remembered its mistake and will eagerly rectify it.

Below: The trainee dog is taught to 'Come' with the aid of a long training leash and greatly encouraged to come forward to its handler by gesture and voice, followed by profuse praise when the exercise is accomplished.

Right: Praise is particularly important to the young dog and is best given as a tactile reward rather than a tidbit.

'Heel' and 'Sit'

When teaching your dog to walk to heel, it should ideally be striding freely along on your left-hand side with its right shoulder level with your left leg. Have the training collar correctly fitted so that it may be pulled tight to check, or allowed to fall slack, at will. The collar should be attached to the training leash and the spare length of leash gathered up in your right hand. The leash in your right hand should be level with your waist and should have a slight loop in it so that there is no tension on the training collar.

To commence this exercise give the command 'Heel' in a firm voice and lead off with your left foot, simultaneously giving a slight jerk with the leash. Make your strides short and bouncing and maintain a brisk pace, encouraging your dog to keep close by patting your left thigh or clicking your fingers. You could carry a small toy or a favorite food treat in your left hand to keep your dog's full attention. Try to avoid hand contact with your dog during heeling training – it might duck away and become hand-shy, a habit which is difficult to cure. Keep your dog constantly alert and, if it is inclined to drag behind you, bring it forward by use of the training collar. Give the leash a short sharp jerk to bring the dog level with your leg, repeat the command 'Heel', and keep walking forward. You may

need to repeat this once or twice and, when your dog attains the correct position, give verbal praise.

If your dog persistently pulls ahead of you, you may be tempted to hold it back with a steady pull on the leash. This is a mistake and can only develop into a trial of strength between you and your pet. As soon as your dog pulls forward, give a short sharp jerk on the training collar and, as the dog checks, the collar will release. Once you have learned to do this correctly, you will find your dog quickly responds. Before long your dog will have learned that it is more comfortable to trot along evenly at your left side than to pull back or to try to run ahead. When you stop moving, you should train your dog to take a sitting position at your left side, facing forward and with its right shoulder next to your left leg.

To encourage your dog to sit from the walk, give the 'Sit' command while raising the right hand with the leash to keep the dog's head up, and use the left hand on the dog's rump to push this down into the correct sitting position. The 'Sit' command should be given in a firm voice, slightly drawn out and with emphasis on the 't' sound. Always insist on an immediate response in this exercise and do not praise sloppy results when the dog swivels around, or rolls over on its back. If this happens, repeat the heeling exercise, walk on a few

Right: Turning at heel is taught in gentle stages with much verbal praise and encouragement.

Left: Young dogs often resent being kept tightly at heel, and first lessons must be aimed at achieving a free striding dog walking level with the handler's left side.

paces, then repeat the 'Sit' command. Try to avoid giving the same commands at identical points in the garden or yard, as it is important to prevent your dog from connecting commands with landmarks.

The dog is taught to sit on command, at any point in any exercise, in the way described above. When your dog sits correctly, and you have praised it, wait for a few moments before giving the release word in a pleased voice and then allow a few minutes of play and relaxation.

Continue heeling by describing large circles to the right and to the left rather than just executing straight lines. When walking a right-handed circle, keep the dog close to your left leg by giving short sharp jerks on the leash and slap your left thigh to give encouragement. Repeat the 'Heel' command at regular intervals, and intersperse the exercise with lots of 'Sit' intervals. Do not reprove bad results in the early days of this exercise. It is quite difficult for the dog to keep close and to move slowly in a circle, and it needs to acquire suppleness in this action. Conversely, you should always praise any semblance of good work. Never continue the lesson if things go from bad to worse; go back to a simple exercise that the dog is bound to do well, give praise, and release it for the day.

Describing the left-handed circle is even more difficult, and the dog will trip you unless you take care. It is easier to walk around a tangible object such as a parked car or a garden pool, if possible, rather than to attempt an imaginary line. Start with the dog at 'Sit'. Give the 'Heel' command and move off briskly with your left foot. If necessary, raise the dog's head over to the left by holding the leash out with your left hand, and use your left leg to ease your dog's head and neck into a left-hand bend. As soon as you are achieving a satisfactory circle, bring in a 'Sit' or two, praise the dog, and end the lesson.

The next day, start with short circles to the right and to the left, adding plenty of 'Sits' at quite different places on the circles. Your dog may start to get sloppy about clean 'Sits' at this time, and this must be corrected. Whenever your dog is slow to assume the 'Sit' on command, or sits in an unbalanced way, tighten up the exercise by over-emphasizing lifting of the dog's head with the leash in the right hand and pushing the rump with the left hand, giving extra firmness in the 'Sit' command. If lax exercises are allowed to pass, they may become bad habits which are difficult or impossible to cure at a later time. Practice heeling daily and vary them between straight lines, right-hand and left-hand circles, zigzags, serpentines, and squares with sharply angled corners.

'Sit and Stay'

Once your dog sits well on command and no longer needs the additional aids of leash and hand pressure, you are ready to start teaching the 'Sit and Stay' exercise. First make the dog 'Sit' in the usual way, then, letting the slack part of the leash droop to the ground, change the end of the leash from your right hand, holding it near the dog's face, and give a firm 'Stay' command. Repeat the word and, holding the hand towards the dog take a long step to the right, extending the left hand so that the leash does not draw the dog towards you. The dog should remain seated, watching you. Repeat the 'Stay' command and reverse your step until you are again placed next to your dog. If your dog remains still, praise it and repeat the exercise once or twice more. If the dog does move, put it back in position and try again Punish any movement with a stern rebuke 'No' and replace the dog with the 'Sit' command.

Repeat the exercise daily and, when your dog is ready, develop it in stages. First loop the end of the training leash on to the left thumb and with the dog in the 'Sit' position give the 'Stay' command; take the usual long step to the right; fully extend the left arm so

that the hand is above the dog's head, then, using the left thumb as a point of pivot, walk slowly in a counter-clockwise direction around your dog until you are back to base. Your dog must not move. If it does, start again from the beginning, even reverting to the original 'Sit and Stay' position if necessary. When you finally achieve a positive result, give lavish praise and release your dog.

You should work the 'Sit and Stay' exercise into your usual daily heelwork routine, together with random 'Sits' until your dog is obviously enjoying the random nature of its exercises. Once you are confident that your dog will stay in 'Sit' while you circle, you can try 'Stay' without the leash. First of all, try putting the end of the leash on the ground while you take your long step to the right. If this is successful, try walking around your dog, returning to the training position. Your dog should remain motionless; if it does not you must return to a previous stage in your program and work up to 'Stay' once more.

The final stage is to remove the training leash while the dog is at 'Sit and Stay' and to walk away. Always take a long side step first to prevent your dog thinking that it is expected to go forward at heel. At this stage

Above left: The handler then gives the 'Stay' command and takes a step to the right.

Above: Repeating the 'Stay' command and reinforcing this with hand signals, the handler moves in a circle around the dog, which must remain at the 'Sit' position.

Left: In teaching 'Sit and Stay' the dog is first taught to sit correctly at the handler's left side and to remain alert.

Right: As the circle is completed further hand- and voice-reinforced signals are given until the handler returns to the starting position.

your dog should connect a forward step with your left foot as being an invitation to heel, while a sideways step away indicates your wish for it to remain motionless.

Take only a few paces away from your dog during the first 'Stay' lessons so that it is not tempted to go forward. Keep repeating 'Stay' in a calm and reassuring voice. Return to the training position before giving praise, then continue with a new exercise or give the release. Vary the procedure so that the release is never anticipated. Be sure that your dog always waits for the next instruction. The end of this exercise indicates an important stage in your dog's training program for it will now realize that the 'Stay' command always means that you are going to return to its side. Good behavior at this time must be lavishly reinforced with praise, while misdemeanors must be punished with a firm 'No' followed by the replacement of your dog in the correct position.

'Wait' and 'Come'

When you wish your dog to remain in a static position and then to come to your side when you call, you must teach a different word to avoid confusion. 'Wait' is an important command which must be carefully taught from the beginning. Sit your dog in the normal way, then move in front of it. Place your right hand in front of the dog's face, showing the palm, and say 'Wait' in a slow low voice. Holding the end of the training leash, back away from the dog while it stays, and repeat the 'Wait' command, then jerk the leash and say 'Come'. When the dog reaches you, praise it and encourage it to sit facing you. If the exercise goes well, reinforce with a repeat. If the dog comes forward as you reverse, start from the beginning again and persevere until you achieve a positive result. If you think the 'Sit' position is about to be relinquished by your dog, pre-empt this by giving the 'Come' command before the dog actually lifts its haunches. Build this exercise in gradually with the other training routines and be sure to avoid boredom. You may replace your training leash with a long thin cord so that you can retreat to a considerable distance while your dog is at 'Wait', and before giving the 'Come' command. You may also add a special tidbit to verbal and manual praise for good results. Eventually, of course, your dog will carry out this test, like the other exercises, off the leash.

'Down' and 'Stay'

You may teach your dog to lie down on command by pulling the lead forward, while saying 'Down' in a low voice, and you may even have to get down with your dog at first. The dog's forelegs may be drawn forward, if it is reluctant to go down, and when the dog has achieved the correct position give lots of praise. Take several days introducing this exercise and once the dog assumes a good 'Down' position on command, proceed to the 'Down and Stay' routine. This is taught in the same way as the 'Sit and Stay' exercise, using a loosely looped leash, stepping away first to the right, then circling the stationary dog. Praise the dog only when it remains in the desired position. If it moves, start again from the beginning of the exercise. Never recall your dog from the 'Down' position for this must be fixed in its mind as a stationary pose to which you will return and give the release. 'Down' and 'Stay' are always static positions, while 'Wait' warns the dog that another command is to follow.

At the time of mastering 'Down and Stay' your dog will have reached an acceptable level of elementary training, and the preceding exercises should be practised and reinforced until your dog happily carries them out gaily and with enthusiasm. Refine the 'Down' command for this is one that may well save your dog's life in an emergency, enabling it to be controlled even at a considerable distance when a dangerous situation may arise. A dog can be commanded to go down at the side of a busy street, in a crowd or during a storm. The well-trained dog will obey without question.

'Leave'

Another potentially life-saving command is 'Leave'. The object of this exercise is to train your dog to leave an object or quarry alone until you release the dog with a further command.

The best way of teaching 'Leave' is to have your dog's favorite treat available and within its reach, but to prevent your dog from touching the treat until you say it is alright to do so. Have the dog on its training collar and leash and start with it in the 'Sit' position. Show your dog the treat, say 'Leave', and put the treat just out of the dog's reach. As the dog tries to take the treat repeat 'Leave' and give a sharp jerk on the leash. Use a different release word for this exercise. If your dog's normal release is 'OK', try 'Paid for' or 'Fetch it' to release it from the 'Leave'. Once your dog has learned to respect the 'Leave' command, the exercise may be extended. The treat may be a biscuit rolled temptingly past the sitting dog's feet, and the dog must not move to take the treat until verbally released.

'Leave' is useful in preventing dogs from being stung by bees and other insects, from digging up your favorite plants in the garden, and from stealing tidbits from the table. The important aspect of this command is that your dog responds instantly to the instruction, and waits for a following command.

The 'Down and Stay' is a similar exercise, except that here the dog is put in the full 'Down' position, before the handler takes the initial sideways step, and completes the full circle, repeating the 'Stay' command and reinforcing this with the hand signal.

Retrieving

The dog's inherent instinct to retrieve dates back to its wild state when it was required to carry its prey back to its lair to feed its young. In the domesticated dog, this natural trait has been developed, and the animal may be trained to carry all manner of articles. Small puppies should be encouraged to carry articles around the house, and should never be scolded for lifting their toys and moving them from place to place. Some breeds, notably those in the gundog group, have a natural flair for retrieving, and may prove easier to train than breeds from the other groups.

To teach your dog to retrieve, have it sitting on your left side and replace the training leash with a long cord. Throw out a suitable article, such as a special training dumb-bell or a piece of smooth wood of similar size and weight. Give the command 'Fetch' in an encouraging tone of voice and allow the dog to run forward to pick up the article. Once this occurs, gently pull on the cord while giving the 'Come' command, take in the slack cord and move a few paces backwards, drawing your dog towards you. When the dog is facing you, tell it to 'Sit' and give praise. Then take the article with one hand on either side of the dog's mouth, give your chosen command, such as 'Drop it' and gently take it from your dog's jaws. Take care not to injure or bruise the dog's mouth, but insist on being allowed to take the retrieved article. Once you have it, praise your dog once more. The dog should then be placed in the 'Heel' position before the lesson is repeated. As this skill develops the distance may be extended, and when the technique has been mastered on the leash, the exercise is continued off it.

If your dog retrieves the article, then decides to race around with it rather than bringing it back to you, you should encourage the dog to come by clapping your hands, calling and perhaps backing away and, as soon as the dog is close, give a firm 'Sit' command. It may also happen that your dog starts to return with the retrieved article, then stops short. Again take a few backwards steps to encourage it to come in close. Some dogs habitually drop the retrieve at the trainer's feet instead of presenting it to the hand. In this case you must replace the article in the dog's mouth with the command 'Hold' or 'Hold it'. Place your hand under the dog's chin and lift it slightly to assist in holding the article. Eventually your dog will realize that it must hold until given the command to relinquish the retrieved article.

As your dog improves its performance you will be able to discontinue the backwards steps and you and your dog will enjoy developing the exercise into more sophisticated procedures such as 'Seek and Find'. Some dogs dislike retrieving hard items like dumb-bells or sticks and prefer to bring back a soft toy or a soft slipper. Great patience is needed to perfect the retrieve, and care must be exercised at all stages, as your dog may misunderstand chastisement for dropping the article during a retrieve and come to resent the entire exercise. The secret of success is to take each stage slowly and methodically, regressing to an earlier stage when things go wrong, and finishing each session on a positive note.

Above: Great attention is given to accustoming the dog to the sight, smell and feel of the dumb-bell used as the retrieve object.

Right: The dog is encouraged to hold the dumb-bell, correctly balanced in its mouth, and to release it into the handler's hands when asked to do so.

Far left: Retrieving is a natural progression from the dog's normal behavior of carrying objects in its mouth. First the training collar must be checked as it should be prior to every exercise.

Left: The young dog is correctly positioned before teaching the 'Retrieve.'

Training to the car

A dog should be accustomed to car travel from early puppyhood if it is to become a happy traveler. From the start take your puppy with you on all your short journeys to the post office or the store. Cover the seats with newspaper and an old towel to protect against possible 'accidents'. Allow three hours to elapse after a meal before taking your puppy on a trip, and encourage it to relieve itself before setting out. It is a good idea to put a puppy in the car from time to time without actually going anywhere. Make sure the windows are slightly open, to allow a fresh air flow while still preventing the dog's escape, and put the puppy's blanket on the seat and leave it to settle down for a few minutes. Increase the length of time during which the puppy is left in the car, and soon it will look forward to the experience. Train your dog to sit on its allocated seat, or on the floor, during journeys and never allow it to hang its head out of the window as this can lead to badly inflamed eyes.

Car training is quite simple once the dog understands the 'Sit' and 'Wait' commands. Your dog should expect to wait patiently on his leash until told to get in to the car and, once inside, should settle down. It is important to teach your dog to wait inside when the door is opened, too, as it is very dangerous for a dog to leap out of a car as soon as it stops and the passengers alight. Your dog must be given the 'Wait' command when the door is opened, and must sit quietly until you tell it to 'Come', when it should come directly to you and sit at heel.

Many dogs become very possessive about their owners' cars and are left on guard to deter thieves. If you train your dog to guard your car, be sure to provide the special grids which enable the windows to be left partly open, letting in fresh air at all times. Dogs have died in cars with tightly closed windows, due to lack of ventilation and heat exhaustion.

On long journeys, take your dog's drinking bowl and a bottle of water. Plan to stop at regular intervals and take your pet for a short walk before offering a drink. Special mesh guards are available to fit in the rear of station wagons, effectively converting the area into an ideal kennel. If you plan to travel a lot with your dog, or expect to take it on vacation with you, such an accessory would prove invaluable.

Some dogs suffer from motion sickness, and this is generally cured by familiarization gained by making lots of short trips so that the dog becomes accustomed to the vehicle's motion. Travel sickness tablets may be obtained from your veterinarian if necessary, and a dog prone to sickness should not be fed for several hours before embarking on a car journey.

This trio of dogs has been taught
to sit still in the back of the car
even though the door has been
raised and left open.

Dogs which respond eagerly to lessons and enjoy training may be taught to perform party tricks, though you should take care to avoid asking your pet to produce behavior which makes it look foolish or undignified. Tricks must only be taught when your dog has mastered its basic training and is obedient in all situations.

'Sit up'

Tricks are taught by encouraging and rewarding each small stage in the build-up to the desired behavior pattern and, unlike the reward for basic training, which is verbal praise and a pat or two, the reward for a trick performance is generally a small treat or tidbit.

Lots of dogs are taught to 'Sit up', but this is really only suitable for small or medium-sized dogs of compact conformation; long-bodied, short-legged dogs find it difficult to balance while sitting on their haunches, and the large breeds look ungainly. Terriers and Toys often enjoy the 'Sit up' and are generally easy to teach. The puppy should be at least six months of age, and obedient, before starting this trick. Begin by holding a tempting tidbit just out of reach above your dog's head. Say 'Sit up' in a firm, encouraging voice, and lift the dog's chest with your other hand. Find the dog's point of balance and repeat the command, simultaneously giving the reward. The intelligent dog soon grasps the connection between the action and the reward and may 'sit up' without encouragement. Never reward this behavior unless you have instigated it by the relevant command, and avoid encouraging the dog to 'sit up' near the dining table, otherwise it will soon become a meal-time pest.

Other tricks

Other tricks are best performed when developed from your own dog's natural behavior patterns. Watch your dog during play and see how it uses its natural skills. Some dogs naturally roll large balls along the ground, others are natural jumpers. Some breeds instinctively enjoy digging and this can be developed into a 'Hide the bone' trick where the dog is taught to take a play bone or chew-stick and to conceal it under a rug or chair, then to 'Go fetch' the article on a further command.

The dog which enjoys stretching out on its side to rest, or having its belly rubbed, will easily learn the 'Dead dog' trick. This command must be given in a low, drawn-out voice to avoid confusion with 'Good dog' which is always given in a bright, warm voice. In the 'Dead dog' trick, the dog must stretch out on its side with its head on the ground and remain quite motionless until given its release word. 'Roll over' is an extension of 'Dead dog', and dogs may be trained to roll once, to and fro, or continuously over and over, depending on their physique. Some dogs prefer to turn forward somersaults, learned while catching a ball in mid-air and having the behavior cleverly rewarded at the optimum moment by a perceptive trainer. Carrying newspapers or shopping baskets are natural progressions from the basic retrieval training, and the gundog breeds often learn these tricks quite naturally.

All tricks are taught in gentle stages, and each lesson must end with a successful move, no matter how slight. If you experience any setback during training, revert to a previously learned behavior pattern, reward the dog when it performs this, and call it a day. It seems best to teach new behavior in the evening, for the dog appears to sleep on each small success, and brings forward the newly learned experience the following day.

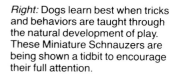

Right: Dogs learn best when tricks and behaviors are taught through the natural development of play. These Miniature Schnauzers are being shown a tidbit to encourage their full attention.

Inset: Learning to 'Shake Hands' is a favorite trick of many dogs which enjoy close contact with their masters.

Left: Many dogs enjoy carrying familiar objects and this trait can be developed into really useful behavior, as seen by this Old English Sheepdog which happily carries his owner's shopping basket.

The destructive dog

Lots of dogs prove destructive in the home and garden during the first year or so. Chewing starts during the puppy's teething stages when it gnaws at all manner of objects to help in cutting its permanent teeth. Because of this, young dogs should never be left for long periods in the home along with valuable items. They may be confined within a playpen while you are out of the house, and given a plentiful supply of toys and chewing treats. Some adult dogs resent being left alone, and scratch timber and carpets in closed doorways. This initial behavior, which is understandable, must be checked to avoid the development of a dedicated canine tearer and chewer. It is pointless to punish your dog for this type of behavior when you return and find the damage. The dog is so pleased to see its owner that it is unable to relate the punishment with the crime, and will perceive the chastisement meted out as retribution for the exuberance of its greeting.

If you must leave your dog for long periods, train it carefully, leaving it for a short while at first, gradually building up the length of time that the animal is alone. Give the dog an interesting environment and a warm, comfortable bed, and make your time together active and enjoyable. Take your dog with you whenever you can, or consider having two dogs which can become good friends.

To retrain a destructive dog, leave it for a short period, return and check for damage. If the dog has started chewing or tearing, make a point of examining the damage, ignoring the dog. Do not punish the dog. Sooner or later you will return and find no damage and this is when you must lavishly praise the animal. The whole process needs plenty of patience and does take weeks or even months before the dog is retrained.

Stealing food

It is very unfair to expect your dog to sit quietly alone in a room with some tempting food and to refrain from stealing. It is a different matter, however, when your dog habitually steals when you are distracted for a moment or two, or grabs food from your worktop or table. When a dog knows the 'Leave' command from basic training, this is employed to halt it in its tracks whenever it looks like taking a tasty morsel. You may also try some aversion therapy by filling a soft candy with mustard before leaving it casually on the table. If the dog notices the candy and looks likely to steal, give the 'Leave' command in a very firm voice and go out of the room. There is a good chance that your dog will take the bait and burn his mouth; two or three experiences like this should effect a cure. If your dog bolts the tidbits too fast to notice the mustard, use larger baits.

Left: Many dogs have naturally destructive habits which must be curbed before they become deep-rooted. It is unwise to allow puppies to play with old slippers as they may be unable to discriminate between the old slipper and the new shoe!
Below: Dogs which habitually steal food must be caught in the act and given a firm 'Leave' command.

Resentment of handling

Some dogs snap when they are groomed or examined, and this is a habit which should be stopped. The problem may arise from unkind grooming, or early abuse of the dog by an ignorant owner or a teasing child. It is important for an owner to be able to handle his dog at any time and in any circumstances. In an accident, for example, this ease of handling could mean the difference between life and death for an injured dog. When a dog first shows signs of resentment to being touched in a particular area you should introduce a familiarization program. First check that there is no injury or pain at the site, then gently touch and stroke the sensitive part while talking soothingly, and praise the dog at the precise moment that it ceases to resist.

If an older dog tries to bite during this training, you must start by using a muzzle. Make sure this fits correctly and is properly made for safety and efficiency. Use the muzzle during ordinary exercise and playtime as well as during the familiarization sessions, otherwise the dog will connect the muzzle with unpleasant aspects of training.

Jumping up

Jumping up at visitors and its owner is natural behavior for a dog. However, because some humans find it unacceptable, it is wise to prevent this behavior by proper training. The younger the dog the easier it is to train. Have your dog on a long training leash fitted to its training collar and set up the situation with a friend. Your assistant should walk in naturally through the door and your dog will bound forward in its usual greeting. Just as the dog starts to jump up, give the leash a really sharp jerk and a stern 'No' command. Follow this with a 'Sit' command, and if this is instantly obeyed, the assistant may praise the dog. This may have to be repeated a few times before the dog appreciates the connection between the punishment and the 'crime'.

If your dog habitually jumps at you, the training collar technique is of little use. The easiest way to stop this behavior is to bring your knee up into the dog's chest just as it jumps forward, and while it is still bemused by your unkind response, give the 'Sit' command, then praise. Once you start to correct jumping-up behavior, insure that your good work is not undone by others actively encouraging your dog up on to its hindlegs.

Barking

Dogs that bark incessantly are intolerable, and they should be retrained before barking becomes a habit. The young puppy is unable to bark at all, and when it first learns to do so it often looks surprised at the noise it has produced. It is tempting, at this stage, to encourage the puppy to bark, but this is a mistake and may prove difficult to correct later.

Most dogs bark only when they feel that their property is threatened, and this is ideal. A dog may bark whenever visitors arrive, but it must be taught that the barking is to stop as soon as you have admitted them to the house. The best way to train your dog is to fit the training collar and leash when the doorbell rings and the dog barks. Then take your dog to the door, and give the 'Sit' command. Open the door and admit your guests while keeping your dog in the 'Sit' position. Punish further barks with a stern 'No' and use of the collar, then allow your guests to greet your dog.

A dog that barks persistently when left alone is difficult to retrain. If a dog begins to bark immediately upon being shut in a room, give a series of stern 'No' commands reinforced by clapping your hands. If this fails, you may admonish the dog, along with the 'No', by shaking the animal's scruff, or even by a short sharp slap. The vital thing to remember is that any punishment must be given within 30 seconds of the bark, otherwise the dog is incapable of connecting the two acts.

Coprophagia

In the wild, dogs eat the droppings of herbivores to obtain roughage and essential nutritional elements. To the human, however, the eating of feces seems quite disgusting, and unacceptable. Most dogs grow out of this habit, especially when they learn that the behavior upsets their owners. The best cure is to keep your dog away from temptation by removing and disposing of feces as soon as they are voided but, if the dog seems obsessive, the veterinarian may prescibe various vitamin and mineral products to be added to its diet.

Bored dogs may get up to all manner of mischief. Keep your dog away from temptation at all times and give it plenty of toys to occupy its attention and prevent boredom.

Basic rules for obedience

NEVER leave your dog alone for long periods during the day – it may get bored and become destructive.

NEVER allow your dog to roam free – make sure your yard gate is closed and that the area is secure.

NEVER leave your dog alone with strange children.

NEVER allow your dog to jump up or scare your visitors, however friendly his intentions may be.

NEVER give your dog a slipper to chew, then punish him for chewing your best shoes.

NEVER fail to inforce a command. It is pointless to say 'No', then to allow your dog to continue the behavior.

NEVER punish bad behavior unless you actually catch the dog in the act, otherwise it will fail to understand your action.

NEVER encourage your dog to chase a bird or any other animal.

NEVER vent your anger on your dog; a verbal reprimand should always be sufficient.

NEVER allow your dog to foul the sidewalk or any area where children play.

NEVER leave your dog alone for long periods during the day – it may get bored and become destructive.

NEVER allow your dog to roam free – make sure your yard gate is closed and that the area is secure.

NEVER allow your dog to jump up or scare your visitors, however friendly his intentions may be.

NEVER encourage your dog to chase a bird or any other animal.

NEVER vent your anger on your dog; a verbal reprimand should always be sufficient.

NEVER allow your dog to foul the sidewalk or any area where children play.

NEVER punish bad behavior unless you actually catch the dog in the act, otherwise it will fail to understand your action.

Diet and exercise

GOLDEN RULES FOR FEEDING YOUR DOG

DO	DO NOT
Feed at regular times	Feed scraps at the table
Insure that fresh drinking water is always available	Feed between meals
Provide suitable feeding bowls for your dog's needs	Wash up your dog's dishes with your own
Check your dog's weight at regular intervals and adjust its food intake accordingly	Let your dog refuse food for more than 24 hours without seeking veterinary advice
Relate your dog's daily ration to its exercise	Leave uneaten food down for your dog to return to later
Cook fresh meat before feeding to your dog to avoid bacterial contamination	Feed any bones except large marrow bones from the shank of beef

A Spaniel puppy contemplates its food possibilities, having to make a choice between milk and cereal, meat and meal, dry food diet, semi-moist diet or assorted biscuits.

Correct feeding

In the wild, dogs eat other animals, consuming the whole of the carcass, including the partially digested vegetable matter in the victim's gut. Each dog gorges itself at the kill, then may go for 48 hours before feeding again. Wild dogs also return to members of the pack unable to hunt – the nursing bitches and puppies – and regurgitate some of the meat to enable them to feed. The domestic dog has a similar digestive system to that of the wild dog, yet seems to cope remarkably well with the unnatural diet on which it is fed.

The pet dog needs regular meals fed at room temperature, and the quantity which should be offered depends on the dog's weight and the amount of exercise it undertakes each day. There are many types of canned meats, dry feed, semi-moist pellets and cereal products produced specifically for dogs – the only problem facing the dog owner is one of choice. Whichever food is chosen, however, every dog needs to have some really hard biscuit each day to exercise his teeth and gums and to prevent the formation of tartar. Fed a correctly balanced diet, your dog will not need extra vitamin pills and additives, but you may find that a teaspoon of corn oil or margarine added to its main meal each day will help to prevent a dull, scurfy coat at molting; and you may add an occasional egg, a dish of cooked liver or some fish to the diet to provide variety.

Make sure you always provide fresh clean drinking water for your dog, and take care to choose bowls and dishes which enable your dog to eat and drink comfortably. Different breeds have different muzzle types, and therefore may need special feeding utensils.

CALORIFIC VALUE OF FOOD REQUIRED BY VARIOUS SIZES OF DOGS

Breed	Average Weight	Kilocalories Per Day
Yorkshire Terrier	5 lb	250
Dachshund	10 lb	450
Beagle	30 lb	900
Labrador Retriever	65 lb	1600
Great Dane	150 lb	3000

ENERGY VALUE OF REGULAR (PROCESSED) DOG FOODS

Food	Protein Content (percentage weight)	Energy Value (kilocalories per lb)
Wheatmeal biscuits	11	1600
Canned meat with jelly	11	400
Canned meat with cereal	8	500
Semi-moist diet	25	1400
Expanded (dry) diet	24	1500

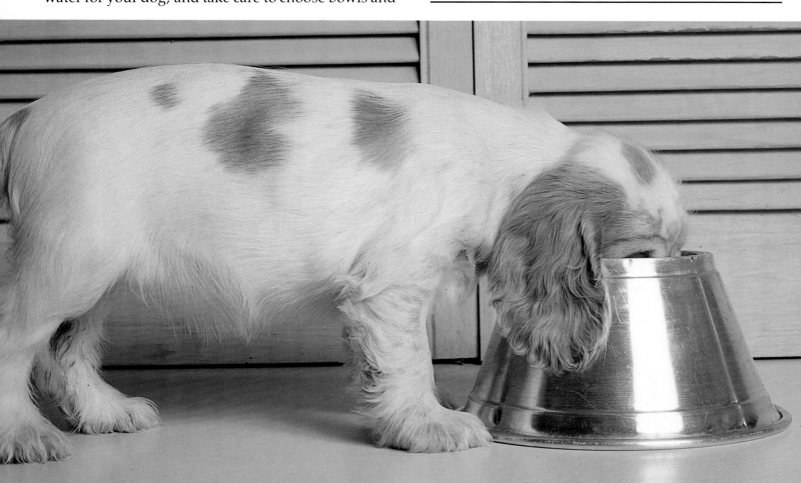

Left: Special dishes and bowls are made for certain breeds and a high-sided bowl is specially manufactured for spaniels, keeping their long ears out of their dinner.

Above: The food intake of every dog should be directly related to its energy requirements. This lively poodle for example, will require more calories than a dog leading a sedentary life.

ENERGY VALUE OF TRADITIONAL (FRESH) FOODS

Food	Protein Content (percentage weight)	Energy Value (kilocalories per lb)
Ground beef	20	1250
Beef liver	21	750
Beef lung (lights)	18	500
Beef spleen (melts)	17	500
Beef tripe	15	450
Whole egg	12	650
Whole milk	3.5	300
Wholemeal bread	9	1000

There are many brands of dog food available and these include canned varieties, some of which are all meat, and some a combination of meat and cereal in various proportions. Most owners find it best to feed all-meat canned food in conjunction with the desired quantity of wheatmeal biscuit. In addition to canned foods there are various types of pre-cooked meats and sausages, sachets of semi-moist pelleted complete foods, and whole diet foods manufactured in the form of concentrated hard pellets.

The amount of food needed depends mostly on the size of the dog and its normal daily activity; young dogs usually require slightly more than normal, whereas old dogs require slightly less. A rough guide to the calorific value of food required by the range of dog sizes, and the energy values of certain dog foods are given in the tables.

The healthy adult dog needs only one main meal a day, but pet dogs are often given a main meal in the morning and a few biscuits at night, or vice versa. Insure that fresh water is always available. Dogs with dietary problems, and those of some of the delicate toy breeds, do better on two or three small meals spread through the day. The dog's digestive system is such that it generally benefits from a large meal of concentrated food rather than a succession of small snacks and it rarely becomes bored with a repetitive diet. Be sure to provide an unlimited supply of drinking water, especially when feeding semi-moist or expanded meal diets.

A bitch fed a normal well-balanced diet will be adequately fed until the fifth week of pregnancy, when she should have an increase in the total volume of daily food, and this should be divided into two equal meals, one given in the morning and one in the evening. By the end of the gestation period, a bitch carrying an average litter of five or six puppies will be consuming about two-thirds more per day than her usual maintenance diet, and a small bitch may be consuming double her normal quantity of food. Just prior to whelping, the bitch will refuse food and may even bring back her last meal. She may take a little milk at intervals during parturition, and some fresh water should be available to her.

Once the puppies are born and beginning to suckle, the bitch will gradually regain her appetite and, during the period of lactation, while feeding a litter of four or five, her daily food requirement will be approximately three times her usual amount, and should be fed in three equal meals, spread through the day. Extra calcium should be added to prevent eclampsia, or milk tetany, which occurs when the puppies drain the bitch's calcium reserves. Cow's milk may be added to the bitch's diet and provides extra calcium in an easily assimilated form, but it can have a laxative effect. Some dog breeders find evaporated milk diluted with an equal quantity of water is more satisfactory. Lactation usually continues until the puppies are about five weeks old. Weaning may start at about three weeks, and the bitch may be 'dried-off' by the time the puppies are six weeks old. As the demands on her are decreased, her demand for food gradually reduces, but if the bitch looks thin after the litter is weaned she must be given extra protein in the form of meat, to replace her lost weight and improve her condition.

During weaning, the puppies need careful feeding to maintain good condition. In nature the bitch would regurgitate partially digested meat from a fresh kill and encourage her puppies to eat this. Breeders may try to copy this by scraping or blending raw meat to a paste, or by soaking pre-cooked cereals in warm milk. Puppies soon learn to lap warm liquids from a shallow bowl or tray and, after a few days, solid food should be introduced. The bitch is kept away from the puppies prior to feeding times, so that the youngsters are hungry when the feed is offered, and this means that they are more likely to accept new tastes and textures. The bitch may be completely separated from the puppies by the time they are six weeks of age. As they grow, the puppies need more and more food, and should have four or five meals spread through the day, and with fresh drinking water available. It is usual to give alternate meals of meat, and cereal with milk. Puppies should always be fed from individual bowls to insure that each always receives its fair share, and added vitamin and mineral supplements should be carefully measured out and added to each puppy's bowl.

At about ten weeks of age, each puppy will be eating well and at this time hard biscuits should be fed separately from the milky component of the diet in order to exercise the teeth and gums and to teach acceptance of a variety of textures. Some breeders introduce raw carrots to add natural vitamins, and some dogs really enjoy crunching fresh vegetables. The number of feeds given per day should be gradually reduced to correspond with the slowing

down of the puppies' growth rates. Some breeds grow rapidly to five months, others keep growing to eight or nine months. Precise quantities of food cannot be prescribed as these also depend on size, growth rates and environment. There is an old saying which holds true today, 'the eye of the master feeds his dog', and it is a simple fact that a dog that looks lean can have its rations increased, while one that looks rotund should have its rations cut back.

Dogs used for breeding need well-balanced nourishing meals to ensure that all their vitamin and mineral requirements are met.

Diet for the growing dog

After weaning, the dog's owner must insure that it receives the correct diet to reach its optimum genetic size and conformation. The young dog may be weighed at regular intervals and its rate of growth compared with published charts for its breed or variety. Adjustments may be made in the amount and number of meals given to bring the puppy's development into line with the average rate. At five or six months, the puppy may have its meal-times reduced to two a day. This is because in the dog, the stomach retains food for some hours. A quarter leaves the stomach four hours after a meal, and another quarter leaves about two hours later, though milk or milky cereal food passes more rapidly through the stomach. At maturity, the dog's nutritional needs decrease and, if fed more than it needs for daily maintenance, the animal will gradually become overweight. Small

Below: Two of the young puppy's daily meals may be of milk mixed to a cream with added cereals, to which a suitable vitamin supplement may be added if required.

Right: The young growing dog needs several small meals each day until it reaches the age of about six months, when two meals should be sufficient.

breeds mature earlier than the large breeds – from seven to ten months as opposed to ten to eighteen months, so the dog owner must be vigilant for signs of maturity, and should cut back the dog's food accordingly. Snacks between meals are to be avoided in the growing dog and care must be taken to insure that the meals fed contain all the vitamins and minerals necessary for laying down strong bones, building strong teeth, and for producing firm muscles, clear skin and a good coat. Vitamins and minerals should be present in their natural form in a good dog diet, otherwise they may be given in the form of a liquid or powder dietary supplement.

The table shows why vitamins and minerals are necessary, and how they may be made available in your dog's diet.

ESSENTIAL VITAMINS

VITAMIN	SOURCE OF SUPPLY	RESULTS OF DEFICIENCY
A	Stabilized Vitamin A oil, liver, liver meal, animal liver meal, corn gluten meal, expanded corn	Poor growth rate in puppies; ophthalmia; lowered resistance to infections of the eyes, mouth and ears, and the respiratory, digestive and urinogenital tracts; reproductive failure
C	Synthesized by the dog in its liver	
D	Cod liver oil, Vitamin D-activated plant sterol	Rickets; poor teeth; poor muscle tone; failure to assimilate calcium and phosphorus
E	Expanded whole wheat, expanded corn, alpha tocopherol supplement	Breeding failure; muscle degeneration; impairment of growth; abnormal lactation
K	Synthesized by the dog in the digestive tract	Blood fails to clot
B Group		
Thiamine	Brewer's yeast, dried skim milk, soybean meal, expanded wheat, expanded corn	Failure to grow; loss of appetite; nervous disorders; paralysis; impaired digestion
Riboflavin	Liver, liver meal, brewer's yeast, dried skim milk, bonemeal, fishmeal	Failure to grow; general weakness; diarrhea; bloodshot eyes; weeping eyes
Niacin	Liver, liver meal, brewer's yeast, dried skim milk, expanded wheat	Nervous disorders; loss of appetite; emaciation; 'black tongue' disease
Pyrodoxine	Liver, liver meal, brewer's yeast, dried skim milk, expanded wheat	Failure to grow; erratic appetite; collapse; coma; convulsions
Choline	Liver, liver meal, fishmeal, brewer's yeast, soy bean meal	Failure to grow; fatty liver; cirrhosis
Folic acid	Liver, liver meal, bonemeal, soybean meal, brewer's yeast	Failure to grow; loss of appetite; reduction of antibody production
B12	Liver, liver meal, fishmeal, bonemeal, dried skim milk	Failure to grow; anemia; liver disorders

ESSENTIAL MINERALS

MINERAL	SOURCE OF SUPPLY	RESULTS OF DEFICIENCY
Calcium	Bonemeal, dried skim milk, dicalcium phosphate	Rickets; bone malformations; hyper-irritability of nerves and muscles
Copper	Liver, liver meal, fishmeal, expanded wheat, trace-mineralized salt	Anemia; diarrhea; fatigue
Iodine	Trace-mineralized salt	Goiter
Iron	Trace-mineralized salt	Anemia; fatigue; diarrhea
Magnesium	Bonemeal, soy bean oil meal, expanded wheat	Convulsions; hyper-irritability
Phosphorus	Bonemeal, dried skim milk, soy bean oil meal, dicalcium phosphate	Rickets; bone malformations; hyper-irritability of nerves and muscles
Potassium	Liver, liver meal, soy bean oil meal, dried skim milk, expanded wheat	Failure to grow; poor muscle tone; restlessness; paralysis
Sodium and chlorine	Liver, liver meal, fish meal, trace-mineralized salt	Reduced appetite; fatigue; exhaustion
Cobalt, manganese and zinc	Trace-mineralized salt	Failure to grow; reproductive problems

Diet and exercise

The health and fitness of the pet dog is maintained by a careful combination of correct well-balanced diet and sufficient healthy exercise. If a dog has been sensibly reared it will accept a wide variety of foods, and the pet can be inexpensively fed by giving a basic diet of a proprietary brand of canned, or lightly cooked fresh meat, mixed with biscuit or meal and supplemented with a variety of household scraps – cereals, milk, cheese, eggs and so on. Dogs should not be given bones from poultry or fish as these may lodge in the throat, or pass down to puncture the intestines. Large beef shank bones, however, provide a means of exercising and cleaning the teeth and gums and also provide some of the calcium and phosphorus lacking in muscle meat. The pet dog may be given the occasional treat, but snacks between meals should be avoided or an obese dog may result. Sweet biscuits and candy bars should also be avoided as these can adversely affect the dog's teeth and digestion. The main meal in the evening should always be given after exercise, the plan being to walk or play with your dog, allow it to cool down and relax, offer a drink of fresh water, then prepare and serve the main meal.

There is no need to attempt to provide the pet dog with an endless variety of flavors, colors and textures in its meals. A dog does best on a regular diet to which its system has become accustomed, and a change of diet or too many additives may result in diarrhea or vomiting. The pet dog, not required to perform any work or to breed, needs a comparatively low calorie diet, though the excitable, hyperactive type of dog will burn more calories than the quiet, docile dog. The dog which plays hard, or accompanies its owner on long hikes or a long jog will obviously use more calories than the dog confined to a yard, or an apartment. Pet dogs can survive and remain quite healthy with very little exercise indeed. Dogs of working breeds, however, may become introverted and lose muscle tone if deprived of a fair amount of exercise, and some may become rather morose or develop neurotic habits such as paw biting or self-licking through lack of exercise and boredom. The majority of dogs benefit from a regular brisk walk once or twice a day. The very large breeds generally need very little exercise, and toy breeds often get all the exercise they require by running around indoors.

When you exercise your pet dog be sure to abide by all the local bylaws. Take with you your own scoop bag to clear up your dog's wastes. Never let your dog off its leash unless you are in a suitably safe environment and you know your dog will return to you whenever you call it. Teach your pet dog to respect other animals, and keep it away from livestock, small children and road traffic.

Right: Each dog should be exercised according to the requirements for its breed or type, and most dogs enjoy a daily game with a ball thrown to encourage them to run and retrieve.

Inset: When playing ball with your dog ensure that it is made of a hard substance which will not disintegrate and be swallowed. The ball itself should be just too large to pass down the dog's throat if taken right into its mouth.

Working dogs need a high energy diet and the correct exercise to build up fitness to perform their various tasks. Some working dogs expend greater energy than others – a sheepdog, for example, uses far more calories in a day than a guide dog, and a breeding bitch needs a higher level of nutrition than a watchdog.

Dogs destined for a working life must be carefully reared from early puppyhood. Great attention must be paid to feeding adequate protein, as well as the minerals and vitamins to lay down a strong skeleton. As the young dog matures, its exercise and training programs must be carefully monitored to develop and build the muscles that it will need to undertake its adult tasks.

Gundogs, hounds and terriers all benefit from long, slow roadwork to build up fitness, to strengthen their backs and legs and to harden their pads. While it is important not to tire the growing puppy, the gradual extension of the exercise periods develops the output and efficiency of the heart and lungs and increases stamina. As the exercising increases, the dog will show an increase in appetite, and will be able to assimilate more food. Its diet should consist of a good quality wheatmeal biscuit, lightly soaked in gravy, with some cooked or canned meat added in a suitable proportion for its type or breed. Dogs used for field work or hunting should be fed early in the evening, then the meal is digested overnight, so that the animal is ready for an early morning start. Dogs used for guard duty should have their main meal in the morning.

The working dog should have its coat and pads examined at the end of each day. The pads should be hard but must not be left overnight with imbedded stones, grit or splinters between the toes. It is important to insure that the feet are clean and dry, and a little lanolin can be massaged into any sore or cracked areas to heal overnight. The dog's coat should be dried if wet and the circulation benefits from a brisk rub down with a suitable brush for the dog's coat type, or with firm toweling. Check ears and eyelids for grass seeds, or awns. Make sure the working dog has a really comfortable warm and draftproof bed so that it can relax and sleep well, ready for a fresh start the following day. In inclement weather, the working dog benefits from added fat in its diet. This can be given in the form of corn oil or margarine.

Right: A Norfolk Terrier performing the task for which his ancestors were first bred – going to ground after its quarry. Working terriers need high protein meals early each evening.

Left: Working dogs like these Collies need high energy diets in order to replace the calories expended during their daily tasks.

Feeding the old dog

Old dogs sometimes suffer from indigestion due to changes in the body. In aging, a gradual reduction of cells and tissues takes place, and not only are the numbers of individual cells in a specific tissue reduced, but they also become smaller, and enzyme activity in the tissues is reduced, slowing the metabolic rate. Renal function and cardiac output are also lower in the old dog than in the adolescent and the young adult. The old dog spends more time sleeping, and needs fewer calories than a younger dog of the same size and breed. Although the old dog needs less calories than a growing puppy, the qualitative value of its diet should be similar. Milk is an ideal way of feeding protein and minerals to the old dog and a variety of cereals can be added to give roughage. The old dog with nephritis needs feeding under veterinary supervision to insure that only sufficient protein to meet its needs is fed, saving undue strain on the functioning of the kidneys. Decaying teeth sometimes affect the appetite and digestion of the old dog, and it may benefit from veterinary extraction of troublesome teeth or a build-up of tartar.

The old dog should be encouraged to take adequate supervised exercise. It should be kept out of the cold and damp, and dried off when necessary. Meals should be small and fed two or three times a day, and the dog should be fed after exercise, never before.

Feeding the sick dog

A sick dog, or one that is in pain following an accident or operation, is unlikely to want to eat. Fasting is beneficial if the animal is vomiting, or is suffering from diarrhea, and one or two days without food does no harm as long as the animal drinks, and does not become dehydrated.

Dogs recovering from illness may need tempting with tasty morsels of nutritious food like pilchard, slices of chicken, cream cheese, morsels of ground beef and egg custard. After anesthesia during which a tube is passed down the throat, the dog may find swallowing painful, and will only accept liquids and puréed foods. You can try proprietary brands of baby food, either meat or milk based, or stir pre-cooked baby cereal oats or rice into warm milk to form a creamy consistency for the dog to lap. Take care with milk products, however, or you may produce loose bowel motions.

Large breeds make poor patients, and are particularly prone to digestive upsets. Any dog which has a tucked up belly and vomits white froth must be given a bland diet for a few days. Try plain boiled rice (the brown variety is better than the white), and add a few cubes of cooked white fish, chicken, turkey or lamb. If the dog will eat charcoal biscuits, these will prove beneficial. The invalid dog should have access to fresh water at all times, and it is best to avoid chlorinated or treated water if possible. Give distilled bottled water, or thawed ice cubes rather than plain water, and make sure that your dog takes all the medicines and additives as prescribed by the veterinarian, and in the correct doses.

Sick and recovering dogs must be carefully exercised according to the veterinarian's instructions. After a period of rest the dog must be lifted or eased to its feet and encouraged to walk around, then to empty its bladder and bowels, too, if necessary. Moving around stimulates the circulation, and may help to increase the appetite. Brushing and gentle massage is also stimulating, and may be carried out before some tempting tidbits are offered. After feeding, allow the dog to rest for 3-4 hours and repeat the exercise.

Left: No matter how friendly the family dogs may be they should always be fed apart and on separate dishes to avoid any possible aggression.

Right: The old dog may need soft food if its teeth have decayed, and requires less calories than a younger dog of the same breed. A warm comfortable bed is essential with plenty of rest periods provided during the day.

Medical care

Dog owners generally show an instinctive recognition of something being wrong with their pet's health or well-being, and this early warning may well save a dog's life. Any definite change in a dog's pattern of daily behavior should be taken as a warning signal, and a careful watch kept for the onset of further symptoms.

It is important to set up and maintain a good relationship with a competent and dog-loving veterinarian from the time a young puppy first joins the household, and to make regular visits for routine checkups and vaccinations throughout the dog's life.

A simple canine first aid kit is inexpensive and easy to assemble and should be easily accessible in case of emergency, and the dog owner should read canine first aid information so that he is ready and able to deal with any dog in distress.

When ill, dogs need warmth, a comfortable bed and peace and quiet to help their recuperation.

Common ailments A-D

Abscess An accumulation of pus caused by a local irritation or infection. The area swells and is painful to the touch. Bathing in comfortably hot water softens the overlying skin, causing the abscess to form a point and eventually burst. Antibiotic treatment effects a rapid cure.

Anal sacs or glands The paired anal sacs lie on either side of the anus, and store liquid produced by them. This liquid gives a characteristic smell to the feces. The sacs may become impacted and fail to empty in the natural way, and thus give rise to local irritation or pain. Your veterinarian will empty the glands when necessary, and will demonstrate this simple manual operation if asked. An affected dog may drag its seat along the ground in an attempt to gain relief, or turn and bite at its tail. If neglected, the anal sacs may become infected, producing yellow pus, when veterinary treatment is needed immediately.

Anemia The condition of the body when there is a deficiency of hemoglobin in the blood. Anemia may follow blood loss after an accident or operation, or infestation with parasites. The cause must be diagnosed and treated without delay.

Arthritis An inflammatory disorder of a joint. There are various types of arthritis due to infection, trauma, etc, but all the causes are not fully understood. Diagnosis is often made by X-ray examination of the affected joint, and though a cure, as such, is not available, relief is afforded with surgery, drug therapy, specialized diet, considerate exercise, and the provision of a soft warm bed.

Babesiosis A protozoan transmitted by the brown dog tick infects the red blood cells and causes this disease, characterized by anemia and jaundice. In the acute form the dog passes coffee-colored urine, becomes feverish and very jaundiced, and dies. In the chronic form the dog suffers general malaise, is slightly anemic and is jaundiced. There is no guaranteed effective treatment, and blood transfusions may be necessary to save a dog with the acute form.

Bad breath This may result from a specific bacterial infection or gum ulcers, from decaying teeth, or from a disease such as chronic nephritis. Often, therefore, bad breath will only be cured by veterinary treatment. It may be corrected by a change of diet (reducing meat content) or a dose of indigestion mixture.

Bladder stones These are fairly common, developing in the bladder of male and female dogs, passing into and lodging in the urethra in male dogs. The affected dog strains to urinate, and only passes small quantities of urine, sometimes bloodstained. There is sometimes some localized inflammation. Surgical removal of the stones is the only successful treatment, and compounds to regulate the acidity of the urine help to prevent the formation of further stones.

Cough This is often a sign of irritation in the throat or bronchial tubes, and may be caused by a foreign body. A persistent cough requires veterinary attention as it could be due to tonsilitis, bronchitis, heart disease, distemper or a highly infectious disease known as kennel cough (infectious canine tracheobronchitis). Dogs can be protected against these last two diseases by vaccination.

Cystitis Inflammation of the bladder characterized by frequent passing of small amounts of urine, and constant straining. It is more common in bitches than in dogs. Water intake must be increased by adding liquid to food. Antibiotic treatment is required; even so the problem may recur.

Diarrhea and enteritis The treatment for simple diarrhea is to withdraw food and drink for 24 hours and to keep the dog warm and quiet. After this the dog should be offered some plain boiled rice with a little chicken stock, and small amounts of boiled water with a little added glucose. If the diarrhea persists longer than 48 hours or the dog vomits, the dog should have veterinary treatment. Parvovirus enteritis is a highly infectious disease which is frequently fatal. First signs are serious vomiting followed by diarrhea, which may be bloodstained. This disease can be prevented by vaccination.

Distemper (hardpad) These are manifestations of a disease caused by a single virus. Starting with a very high temperature, of about 102°F, the dog refuses food and may have diarrhea and a cough, and inflamed eyes. As the nervous system can be affected, the dog may suffer fits. Hardpad is the term used when the virus affects the pads, producing swelling and a leathery feel. Antibiotic treatment controls the enteritis and pneumonia, but most dogs die from the effect of the virus on the nervous system. Vaccination is effective in preventing distemper and hardpad.

Right: The dog's head is held with the chin tilted up and the throat massaged while the pill is swallowed.

Left: Giving a pill is quite easy when the dog's mouth is opened, with the lips held over the top teeth, then the pill is dropped gently at the back of the throat.

Ear diseases Scratching at the ears, head-shaking, or an unpleasant smell may indicate a disease of the dog's ears. Healthy ears are shiny inside, pale pink and free from dirt, wax or debris. Soreness should be reported to the veterinarian, as should any discharge. Parasites known as ear mites live and breed deep in the ear canal. They are eradicated by use of an appropriate parasiticide, while other diseases are dealt with by prescribed drops or ointments, sometimes together with antibiotic and anti-inflammatory drugs given by injection or orally. Trouble in the ears should be treated without delay to save the dog constant irritation or pain.

Eye infections Conjunctivitis is common in the dog and is treated with applications of antibiotic ointments or drops. A partially closed, watering eye may indicate the presence of a foreign body. This should be identified and removed if possible with the corner of a clean handkerchief, or by flushing out with a syringe of warmed saline solution or water. If the object cannot be seen, seek veterinary advice. If there is any damage to the surface of the eye, or a blue effect is noticed, veterinary attention is urgently required. A blue cornea may follow an infection or some types of vaccination. Other causes of blueness in the eye are the formation of a cataract, or a sign of aging in the dog.

Corneal ulcers form on the surface of the cornea. They are painful and affected dogs rub at the eye, while holding it partially closed. The third eyelid may be visible. Eye ointment may effect a cure, though persistent ulcers may need surgical treatment or chemical cauterization.

Fits Intestinal worms are reputed to cause fits in puppies. Preventative measures include regular worming treatments from weaning to six months of age.

Epilepsy causes repeated fits in adult dogs, and the fits usually start soon after the dog attains maturity. A typical fit results in the dog losing consciousness but exhibiting nervous spasms. Any object that might injure the dog should be removed, and the room should be kept dark and quiet until the dog comes out of the fit. Do not open the dog's mouth to prevent choking; it will not help and you might get bitten.

Fleas These small flightless insects which suck the dog's blood have a debilitating effect on the animal and may also give rise to an allergic skin reaction to the bites. The dog flea also acts as host to other parasites, including the tapeworm. Special soaps, sprays, shampoos and powders can be employed to remove fleas from the dog's coat, and treatment should be extended to the dog's bed and to areas in which it rests in order to eradicate flea eggs and larvae which develop off the dog's body in rugs, carpets and house dust.

Gastric torsion Also known as acute gastric dilation-torsion, or bloat, this is a life-threatening condition which occurs most frequently in large deep-chested

Above: The inside of the dog's ear is quite complex and only the visible parts should be gently cleaned during grooming. Trouble in the ear requires veterinary attention.

breeds. Two to four hours after feeding, particularly if exercise follows a large meal, the dog shows signs of pain and distress, with a distended abdomen. Treat it as an emergency needing immediate veterinary aid.

Gastritis The dog with gastritis has an inflamed stomach, indicated first by vomiting or the eating of grass. Keep the dog warm, withdraw food and offer small amounts of cooled boiled water. When inflammation of the bowel also occurs, the result is gastro-enteritis. This may be caused by bacterial or virus infection, or by swallowing an object such as a toy or a rubber band. Veterinary advice is essential and should not be delayed longer than 24 hours.

Heatstroke Confining a dog in a closed vehicle exposed to the sun is the prime cause of heatstroke in the dog, and this can often be fatal. The dog becomes distressed and unable to breathe properly. As the respiration deteriorates and the animal's temperature rises, the dog collapses. First aid treatment consists of reducing the dog's temperature by dipping it in cold water, placing it under a shower or running cold water from a hose pipe over it. A bag of ice placed at the back of the dog's neck, and ice cubes rubbed on the pads will help to get the temperature down. Artificial respiration may be necessary to restore the dog's breathing and heart rate.

Hepatitis An infectious disease caused by a virus. The affected dog develops a high temperature which may reach 105°F, together with sickness and bloodstained diarrhea. Veterinary attention is vital, but may prove ineffective. This disease affects the liver, causing it to become inflamed, and can be prevented by vaccination.

Hip dysplasia This is an inherited deformity of the hip joint, occurring particularly in the larger breeds. Severely affected dogs suffer pain and lameness, and may be treated by drugs or surgery. Dysplastic dogs should not be allowed to breed.

Heartworms see Roundworms, hookworms and heartworms.

Hookworms see Roundworms, hookworms and heartworms.

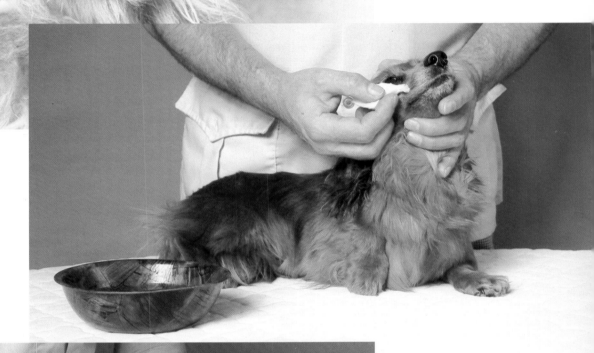

Left: A sore weeping eye . . .

Right: . . . should be gently bathed with cotton swabs dipped into a warm saline solution . . .

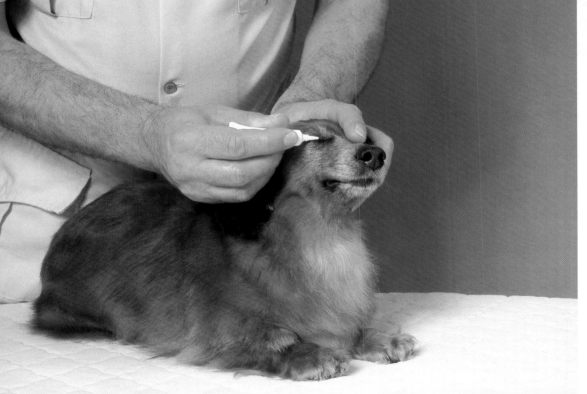

Left: . . . then a soothing antibiotic ointment is administered by squeezing a tiny thread along the lid.

Jaundice Jaundice is a symptom of serious canine disease including leptospirosis and hepatitis. The skin, eyes and mucous membranes become yellow, as does the urine. Urgent veterinary advice is essential.

Leptospirosis This is a serious bacterial infection which can be prevented by annual vaccination. Leptospirosis has a sudden onset. The dog refuses to eat, often becomes excessively thirsty, and may show symptoms similar to those of hepatitis. Death may occur five to ten days after the first symptoms show. Treatment is by antibiotics and fluid drip therapy, and careful nursing is required.

Lice These wingless insects have mouthparts specially adapted for piercing and sucking blood and tissue fluids. The dog louse is species specific, and may be present in large numbers on an affected animal. While the adult lice are easily killed by the application of a suitable insecticide, the eggs, called nits, are not, being hard coated, and cemented to the hair, particularly around the dog's ears. Nits are particularly difficult to eradicate, and the dog should be treated at seven to ten day intervals for several weeks. Lice can cause anemia and can transmit diseases such as babesiosis.

Mites Mites are small parasites related to spiders, which cause irritation of the skin. The odectes mite causes canker of the ear in the dog. Sarcoptic mange is caused by mites which burrow into the skin, causing general thickening and intense irritation. An affected dog becomes increasingly depressed and irritable, and may need intensive treatment. Follicular mange is caused by a microscopic mite which burrows into the hair follicles. In puppies, small patches of hair fall out around the forehead, eyes, muzzle and paws, while in older dogs the hair loss may be more generalized. Extended treatment is required to rid the dog of these parasites.

Nephritis Nephritis, or inflammation of the kidneys, results from infection, and the dog can become acutely ill. Though there is no cure for chronic nephritis, feeding a low-protein diet can help, and veterinary maintenance techniques can help the dog to lead a happy life unless it has suffered extensive kidney damage.

Pneumonia Difficult or distressed breathing accompanied by general malaise and a raised temperature indicates pneumonia in the dog. Urgent veterinary attention is essential.

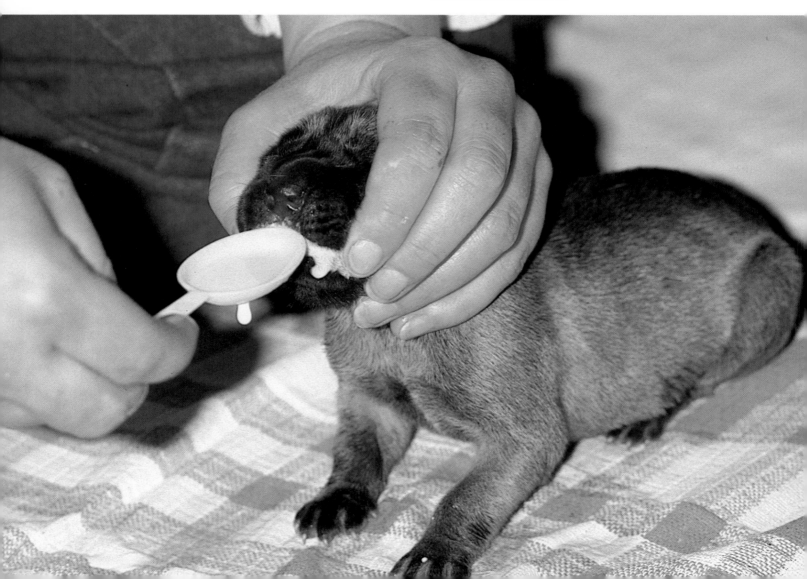

Poisoning Dog owners should make themselves aware of the address and telephone number of their nearest Poison Control Center for emergency use. Different poisons produce different symptoms in the dog, and it is helpful to determine which poison a dog might have swallowed. If the dog has been observed recently taking poisoned bait, force it to vomit by feeding a strong solution of six teaspoons of salt to a glass of warm water. After it has vomited, feed the dog several egg whites and seek urgent veterinary help. When the poison is unidentifiable, waste no time in seeking aid.

Porcupine quills In a confrontation between a dog and porcupine, the dog comes off worst and may end up with innumerable quills imbedded in its face, neck and forelegs. Removal of the quills is painful, and the application of warmed vinegar helps to soften them. Pliers must be used to gently ease the quills from the dog's skin, and veterinary help may be needed to avoid excessive pain to the dog.

Below left: Following a serious illness, the dog may be encouraged to take small quantities of nourishing food from a spoon.

Below: The dog's temperature is taken by inserting a veterinary thermometer in its rectum. The rectal temperature in the normal resting dog is 101.5°F.

Above: When dog meets porcupine it is the latter that generally wins and the dog needs veterinary treatment to remove the many painful quills embedded in its face and legs.

Rabies This dreaded disease is caused by a virus transmitted by contact with infected saliva, usually from the bite of a rabid animal. Every mammal is susceptible to rabies and wild animals have been found to be reservoir hosts. In the United States these hosts are particularly the skunk, the fox, the raccoon and bats, both indigenous and migratory. Dogs are the primary direct source of rabies in man and, happily, there are rabies vaccinations which protect dogs against this disease for up to three years.

A dog infected with rabies may suffer convulsions, snapping and biting at any object or person, and will refuse to drink. One of the first symptoms in the dog may be a sudden and evident fear of its owner. Later the dog becomes dehydrated, then paralysis sets in, followed by death. A suspected rabid dog should be confined in a room away from people and other pets whilst veterinary assistance is instantly sought.

Rheumatism Localized pain in the limbs may be caused by muscular rheumatism which is eased with specific drugs and the provision of a warm comfortable bed. Gentle regular massaging of the affected limbs is also beneficial.

Rickettsial disease Salmon poisoning occurs in the Pacific Northwest where dogs take salmon from streams and rivers in which the fish spawn. Salmon and some trout carry larvae of the salmon fluke which in turn carry a micro-organism which causes the disease. Affected dogs run a high fever, then the temperature drops to subnormal over a period of seven to ten days during which time the dog is severely depressed and refuses food. The dog drinks copiously, vomits and has diarrhea (often bloodstained), and quickly becomes emaciated and dehydrated. The mortality rate is high, though veterinary treatment may be effective if started early enough.

Another disease caused by a rickettsia-like organism is canine ehrlichiosis, which occurs in two forms, one of which is seemingly related to the German Shepherd. Introduced into the dog's system by a tick bite, the disease starts mildly over a period of about three weeks during which the dog loses its appetite, runs a fever and has ocular and nasal discharge. In this acute phase, veterinary treatment is often effective. In the German Shepherd, a chronic phase occurs, and there is a dramatic decrease in red and white blood cells and

platelets to a critical level. Hemorrhage, anemia and extreme susceptibility to other infections occur, and blood transfusions may be necessary to save the dog.

Ringworm Caused by a fungus that parasitizes the skin, ringworm is more common in the shortcoated breeds of dog. The disease is identified by laboratory tests on skin scrapings and examination under ultraviolet light. Dogs with ringworm generally have characteristic lesions that appear as roughly circular and scaly, and the hair is broken off leaving stubby ends. There may also be pustules, or crusty scabs in the affected areas. Ringworm is highly contagious and transmissible to man, so systemic treatment is required. The dog is treated with oral drugs and topical skin dressings. Its bedding should be burned and its living accommodation thoroughly disinfected with a suitable antifungal preparation.

Roundworms, hookworms and heartworms
Roundworms are internal parasites and very common in puppies. The eggs hatch in the intestines, and the microscopic larvae burrow through the liver and lungs. After developmental changes they migrate into the intestines where they reach maturity and lay eggs, repeating the life cycle. A heavy infestation of roundworms debilitates the dog. Affected puppies may eat excessively, and have diarrhea and a characteristic pot-bellied appearance. Treatment consists of giving tablets at ten to fourteen-day intervals to eradicate the worms present in the intestines.

Hookworms are common in puppies and should be treated without delay, for a heavily infected dog soon becomes weak and anemic. Treatment must be undertaken under strict veterinary control, and the dog sometimes requires a blood transfusion before the worming medicine may be administered.

Heartworms, as the name suggests, invade the dog's heart, entering the right side of the organ and the pulmonary arteries. This parasite is spread by biting insects. A dog affected by heartworm tires easily, has a chronic cough and loses weight. A blood test shows the presence of the parasite and intravenous drugs are given to eradicate it. In mosquito areas, oral medications may be given to prevent infection with heartworm.

This eight week old Irish Setter puppy must be protected against disease by vaccination and should also be treated for possible infection by common intestinal parasites such as roundworms.

Shock Any trauma can produce a state of shock in the dog. The symptoms may include apparent fear, a marked paleness or blanching of the mucous membranes or complete prostration. The dog should be placed in a quiet darkened environment and kept very warm until help is at hand. Veterinary attention is required without delay.

Skunk odor A confrontation between a dog and a skunk often leaves the dog covered with an obnoxious odor. This is difficult to remove, but an effective treatment is to rub a large can of tomato juice into the entire coat, working it well into the skin. Follow this with a regular bath with tepid water and a good shampoo. If the odor still lingers, repeat the process.

Tapeworms Two species infest the dog, *Dipylidium* which spends part of its life cycle in the flea, and *Taenia* which spends part of its cycle in the rabbit, cattle or sheep. In order for a dog to be infected with tapeworm, it has to ingest an infected flea, or the infected viscera of one of these host creatures. The tapeworm rarely makes its presence known until small segments looking like live grains of rice are seen near the animal's anus, or on its bedding. Various drugs are available to eradicate the worm, and reinfestation should be prevented by keeping the dog free from fleas and away from rabbits and raw offal.

Warts These are common in older dogs, particularly spaniels and poodles. They are normally benign tumors and are caused by a virus which is highly specific for each host species. Infectious warts usually appear in multiple clusters, especially around the lips and mouth, and cause great inconvenience in feeding. Warts may cause problems or look unsightly; therefore they may be surgically removed. Treatment with specific vaccines has not proved very effective in preventing the spread of warts. The vaccines are those of the autogenous variety, made from a suspension prepared from warts of an affected dog, then injected back into the animal.

Weight loss A gradual loss of weight in the dog may mean that too little food is being given. Step up the quantities in your dog's diet and see if the problem resolves itself. A loss of weight may be the first symptom of a serious disease such as cancer, diabetes, nephritis, pancreatitis, or tuberculosis, or could indicate infestation with parasitic worms. Sudden weight loss should be investigated by the veterinarian.

Whipworms These parasites inhabit the large intestine (and cecum) of the dog. Symptoms of infestation include intermittent diarrhea. Seek veterinary assistance if you suspect this ailment.

An underweight and probably worm-infested feral dog, pictured in the Valley of the Kings, in Egypt. Such dogs live off meager scraps and similar dogs may be found in many of the world's cities, even in affluent nations.

Recognizing illness in your dog

The caring owner has an instinctive feeling for his dog, and senses the moment that it is off color or not functioning in its normal manner. Even so, many dogs become sick and, for one reason or another, early symptoms pass unnoticed. A dog's normal behavior patterns should be carefully noted. Dogs sleep a great deal, but during their periods of wakefulness they should always be alert. A dog that is normally lively and playful, but becomes suddenly listless, is almost certainly incubating a disease or has suffered an injury. As dogs grow older, or a bitch's pregnancy advances, you can expect a gradual slowing down, otherwise take heed, and check for problem areas.

Acute diseases develop rapidly in the dog and distinct symptoms soon become obvious; in chronic diseases the onset if often insidious and symptoms may go unnoticed.

HEALTH CHECKLIST

SIGNS OF HEALTH	SIGNS OF ILLNESS
Bright eyes	Sore, ulcerated or dull eyes
Clear eyes	Discharging eyes
Cool, moist nose	Warm, dry or discharging nose
Fresh-smelling mouth; pink gums	Foul-smelling mouth; pale gums

The healthy dog has bright eyes, a cool moist nose and a glossy coat. This dog has all those features but is carrying too much weight.

Clean white teeth	Discolored teeth
Ears clean and pink inside and fresh smelling	Ears dirty with dark deposits or foul smelling
Body clear of lesions or inflamed patches	Body showing wounds, inflammation or areas denuded of hair
Comfortable stance and movement	Hunched attitude, stiffness of movement
Loose elastic skin which springs back when lifted away from the dog's body	Taut skin which stays crimped when lifted away from the dog's body
Rectal temperature of 101.5°F	Raised or lowered temperature

ILLNESS DIAGNOSIS CHECKLIST

SYMPTOM	POSSIBLE CAUSE
Shaking the head	Ear disease
Hanging the head to one side	Foreign body in ear
Scratching at ear	Irritation or parasites in the ear or on the ear flap
Drooling	Foreign body in the mouth or throat May mean rabies
Pawing at mouth	Foreign body lodged in teeth or across the palate; insect bite; toothache
Discharging nose	Foreign body; serious disease such as distemper
Flatulence	Incorrect diet
Dragging seat along ground	Impacted anal glands
Yellowing of skin and mucous membranes	Jaundice
Scratching	Parasitic infection; fungus infection; incorrect diet; allergy
Refusal to eat	
Excessive thirst	
Lethargy in normally active dog	
Vomiting froth or bile	
Sudden weight loss	Any of these symptoms may signal the onset of a serious disease
Diarrhea (for more than 24 hours)	
Coughing	
Dehydration	
Gradual swelling of abdomen	Pregnancy; false pregnancy; overfeeding; dropsy tumor
Sudden swelling of abdomen in a large breed, after feeding	Gastric torsion EMERGENCY
Swollen breast	Mammary tumor; mastitis
Swollen testicles	Injury; testicular tumor or infection
Blood from penis	Injury; cystitis; urolithiasis prostatitis EMERGENCY
Discharge from penis	Local infection
Blood from vulva	Estrus; cystitis; urolithiasis; injury
Discharge from vulva	Vaginitis; pyometritis

Visiting the vet

It is important to get to know your veterinarian when your dog is in good health, and this is done by making appointments for regular health checks from early puppyhood. The first visit will be to have the new puppy thoroughly checked and to institute a program of vaccinations and worming. The veterinarian will then take an interest in the progress of the puppy and the young dog will remember the kind and gentle treatment received in the sensitive period of its development. There may come a time when you need the vet in an emergency situation, and it is helpful if he already knows you, your dog and its health record and particulars. Always make firm appointments for routine veterinary care, and take your dog along in good time. Make sure it is fitted with a safe collar and lead, and is clean and well groomed. It is usually a good time to take with you the dog's current vaccination certificates or health record card for updating.

In an emergency situation, telephone the vet's office and keep calm. Give your name and a brief description of the problem, then waste no time in going straight to the location where your dog can receive the necessary help. If the dog has been injured, move it as carefully as possible, sliding it on to a coat or blanket which may be used as a stretcher. Try to get someone else to drive you while you comfort and reassure the dog.

On arrival at the vet's office, be as concise as possible in giving full details of the problem with the dog. Depending on its condition, the veterinarian may want to know details of the accident and its timing, or the time of the onset and duration of serious symptoms. You should be prepared to list the dog's food and liquid intake, in case anesthesia and surgery is necessary. You may be asked about previous illnesses and behavior patterns. Give accurate, succinct answers, and remember that your calm attitude will have a corresponding calming influence on your dog. If you are particularly upset by a clinical environment, or cannot tolerate the possible sight of blood or needles, then it is advisable to ask a friend or relative to accompany your dog for examination and treatment.

Right: The moving of an injured dog must be undertaken with great care to avoid further damage. Use a blanket or towel as a stretcher and seek veterinary help without delay.

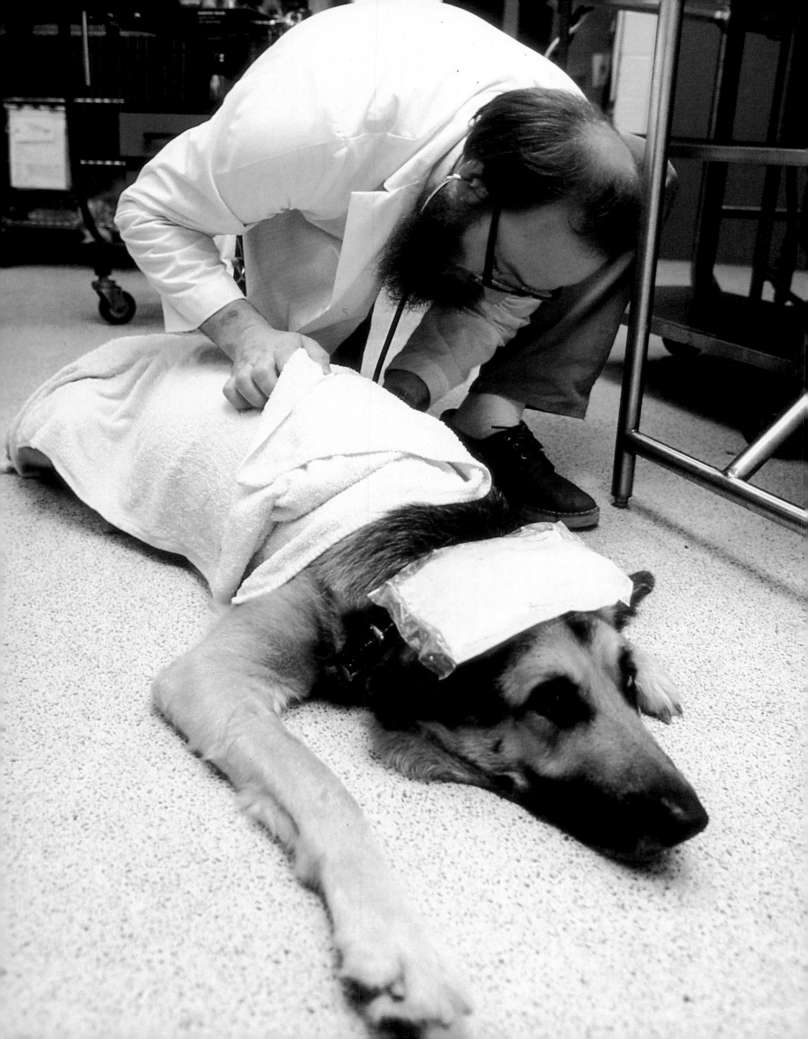

The veterinary office or hospital is equipped to deal with all manner of canine problems, from the simplest routine vaccination to the most complicated of surgical procedures. Operations are carried out with the same skill and precision as used in surgery on humans, with the same considerations for hygiene, pain relief and after-care. If your dog needs a highly specialized form of treatment, or complicated surgery, then you might be referred to another veterinarian more qualified or better equipped to deal with your case.

Many practices employ a team of veterinarians, but it is advisable for you to ask to see the one who generally treats your dog, to ensure continuity. Every vet will do his utmost to treat your dog in the best possible way but, nevertheless, past experience with a particular animal is always helpful in reaching a correct diagnosis and deciding upon the best form of treatment. You should never start a course of treatment with one veterinarian, then seek advice from another. This is unethical, and is not in your dog's best interests. If your dog seems little improved by the treatment it receives, it is up to you to explain this to your vet, and ask him to try something else. If your vet finds that he cannot make any progress with your dog's illness, he may well decide to seek the advice of a colleague, in the form of a professional second opinion. You may also ask for a second opinion if you are not happy with your dog's progress. In stubborn cases specialist advice may be sought and this may produce a fresh approach and more effective treatment.

General veterinary care consists of a thorough health check of the canine patient, with note taken of any signs and symptoms which the owner may have noticed, and of the dog's past history. The vet will check the dog's heart and lungs, its temperature and pulse, and may take a blood sample for laboratory analysis. You may be asked to collect samples of the dog's feces and urine for analysis. The most important piece of information your vet will want to know is of any change in your dog's normal behavior patterns.

If your dog has been injured, it may be bound, bandaged or have a limb put in a cast. Make sure you know how to change dressings, or keep bandages and casts clean and comfortable, and make a firm appointment for a revisit.

If your dog has an illness, you will be given drugs and medicines in various forms. If you are unsure how to give tablets or liquid medicine, ask the vet to show you, for it is important for your dog to receive the correct dosage at the prescribed intervals of time in order to recover. It is not desirable to mix drugs in the dog's food. The dog may refuse to eat the meal, or the drug could lose its potency when mixed with other substances. Dogs are quite easy to dose once you have mastered the technique.

When your dog is started on a course of treatment, especially antibiotics, be sure to finish the whole course of treatment. It is tempting to stop giving the drugs when the dog appears to have bounced back to health, but the treatment consists of an entire course of medicine over a specific time period, and must be completed to achieve the full effect and to prevent a possible relapse.

You should also ensure that you contact your veterinarian to report the satisfactory recovery of your dog. This feedback is rewarding, and positive results may help him successfully to treat other similar cases.

Right: Veterinarians derive a vocational pleasure from helping to return dogs to health and strength after an accident.

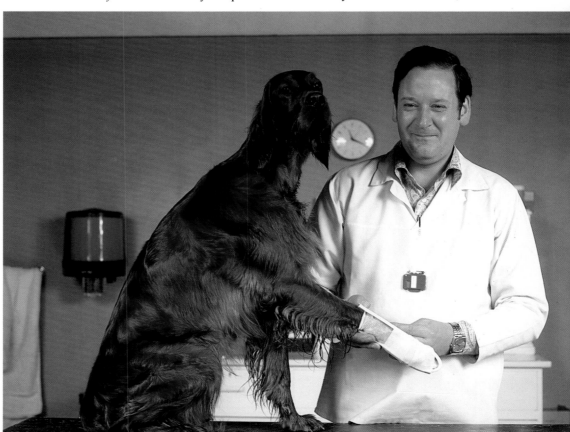

Left: Following a road accident the veterinarian wastes no time in carrying out a full examination and giving emergency, life-saving treatment to the injured dog.

Home nursing

When your dog is seriously ill, the veterinarian will do everything possible to aid its recovery, using injections, transfusions, medicines and tablets as necessary, but the actual process of nursing the animal back to full health is likely to be carried out by you, the owner. Home nursing is an essential part of the dog's recovery program. It is carried out under veterinary guidance, and is aimed at alleviating as much discomfort, pain and distress as possible.

A comfortable bed is the first consideration. It must be large enough to allow the dog to stretch out and should be of an impervious, easily cleaned material such as a hard plastic. The best bedding is a thick pad of polyester fur cut to fit the bed. This material is ideal for the sick dog as it is easily washed and quickly dried and any liquid or urine goes straight through the pile, leaving the surface next to the animal's skin warm and dry. Have two pads, so that you always have a fresh clean replacement at hand. If the patient is unable to move around, lift the dog carefully and turn it to lie on the other side, repeating this process every hour or so to prevent the formation of sores on the pressure points. If the dog is capable of movement, but must be restrained, you should procure a pen and place this around the bed. The room in which the dog is nursed should be kept comfortably warm and well ventilated. A dull-emitter infra-red heat lamp suspended at a safe height over the bed proves beneficial and comforting.

Fresh drinking water is essential, and must be available to the dog at all times. If it is unable to lap, you may dribble water from a clean sponge into the dog's mouth. You might find that your dog will accept milk diluted with a equal volume of water when it refuses plain water. If it proves impossible to give fluids by mouth, the dog will be put on a fluid drip apparatus by the vet. The sick dog may well lose its appetite and need coaxing to eat. Force-feeding will only result in vomiting and this may induce dehydra-

tion. Try offering tiny tidbits of meat, fish, shrimp, hard-boiled or scrambled egg, or cottage cheese. As the patient progresses, institute a gradual return to its normal favorite diet.

Urination and defecation may be a problem, particularly in the totally incapacitated dog. If the dog is quite unable to move around, then disposable diapers, as made for human babies, should be used to collect wastes. Urination may be stimulated by gentle pressure on the abdomen – the vet will show you how. Defecation may take place infrequently in the immobile dog. You should change the diapers frequently, wash and dry the genital and rectal areas, and apply talcum powder to keep the region fresh and dry. If the dog is able to walk, take it out every four hours and encourage it to relieve itself in the normal way. Keep a record of the dog's urination and defecation in case veterinary help is required.

Keep the canine patient's coat clean and free from knots by gentle grooming. Use a damp sponge around the eyes, nostrils and lips, and a separate sponge for cleaning the genital area. If the dog has congested lungs or a discharging nose, inhalation of hot vapors may prove beneficial.

In nursing post-operative cases, take the greatest care that your dog does not put any strain on the wound, its stitches or sutures. Even if the dog is going outside to urinate, put it on the leash to prevent any sudden or excessive movement which might affect the wound. Scold your dog if it shows any inclination to bite at the stitches or lick the site of the operation. A bandage or Elizabethan collar may be helpful. Should any stitches be removed, or the incision show signs of discharge, call the vet immediately.

In home nursing, the dog must be made comfortable and kept warm, clean and calm. Medications must be administered with the minimum of fuss, and gentle brushing and combing may instil a feeling of well-being in the sick animal.

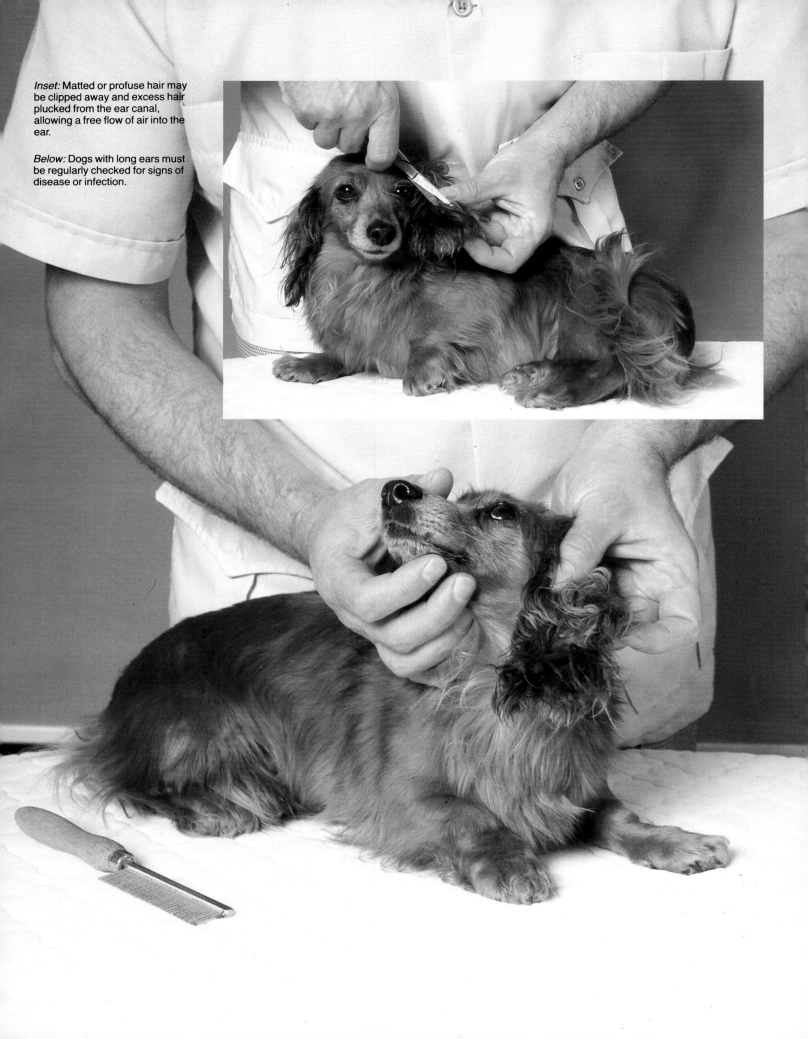

Inset: Matted or profuse hair may be clipped away and excess hair plucked from the ear canal, allowing a free flow of air into the ear.

Below: Dogs with long ears must be regularly checked for signs of disease or infection.

The eyes

You may need to wipe away small deposits from the inner corners of your dog's eyes. Use moistened cotton wool or tissues, and take a fresh piece for each eye. Some dogs have drooping lower eyelids, and these constantly water, staining the area below the eyes. If this is excessive, seek veterinary advice. A thick discharge from the eyes indicates an eye infection which possibly needs antibiotic ointment or drops to clear it up.

The ears

Erect ears present few problems and are best checked weekly and wiped out with moistened cotton wool or tissues. Do not probe the ear canal, just clean away any light waxy deposits, grease and dust. If there is a dark discharge, or a smell from the ear canal, seek veterinary attention.

Long drooping ears can pose problems, especially if there is also a growth of hair on the inside of the flaps. This should be clipped away in the summer months to prevent it collecting grass seeds and awns. Poodles and certain other breeds are prone to developing a thick growth of very fine hair in the ear canal. This should be regularly plucked to allow air to pass into the ear, otherwise serious ear problems can occur. Any sign of disease or infection in the dog's ears should receive immediate veterinary treatment; home treatment with cream, lotions and powders may aggravate the condition. The constant discomfort and eventual pain will depress the dog, probably causing behavioral problems, and could eventually result in the need for surgery.

Below left: The dog's claws should be kept worn down to ground level or may be cut back with clippers.

Below right: A Dalmatian has its teeth checked for a buildup of tartar.

The mouth

The dog's mouth and teeth should be clean and healthy and, if you start at an early age, you can teach your dog to enjoy having its teeth cleaned. A normal, medium-hard toothbrush is used with plain water to clean away food particles and debris from between and behind the teeth. Feeding the dog hard biscuits helps to prevent the build-up of tartar on the teeth and gums, and also helps prevent gingivitis. Tartar and gingivitis are prime causes of bad breath in dogs. A weekly check of your dog's mouth will ensure that you do not allow tartar formation and subsequent tooth loss. Give the occasional large shank bone, rawhide chews and hard biscuit to exercise the teeth and gums, and this will not only keep the mouth healthy and the breath fresh but will aid digestion and produce a healthier, happier dog.

The feet

The pads of most dogs get a tremendous amount of wear and tear, but very little care from the average owner. A caring owner will check the dog's feet after exercise to make sure no tiny stones or other foreign bodies have lodged between the toes, and that there are no abrasions or cuts. Dogs with long tufts of hair between the toes should have the tufts clipped back to prevent them matting. Some dogs are prone to the development of interdigital cysts – painful little swellings between the toes which bother the dog, causing constant licking and a degree of lameness. These cysts need veterinary attention. Claws should be kept worn down to ground level by proper exercise on hard ground. If the claws grow too long, have them professionally clipped or learn to do this yourself. Use only nail clippers and avoid cutting into the sensitive quick. Clip the dew-claws, too, if these are present, to prevent them growing round and back into the skin.

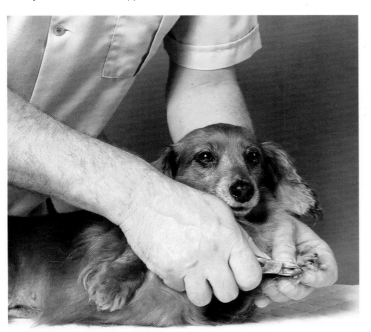

Grooming is an essential part of the dog's daily or weekly routine, and should be instituted in puppyhood, so that it is an accepted and enjoyable part of your dog's life. The diverse range of coat lengths and hair types in the canine kingdom has led to a bewildering range of brushes, combs and grooming aids being available on the market, and it is important to select and use the right tools for your own dog. Always buy proper equipment for grooming your dog; brushes and combs made for human hair are rarely suitable. If you have a pedigree puppy, the breeder will give you valuable advice on grooming tools and aids; otherwise ask for advice in the pet store. Generally speaking, dogs with short close coats need grooming daily with a good quality short-bristled brush. Used in long sweeping strokes in the direction of the hair growth, this will stimulate the circulation, giving an overall glow to the coat while removing dust, dirt and dry flakes from the skin, and taking out dead hair. Take care around the delicate regions like the head and the genital area.

Long coated dogs need careful combing to separate the hairs right down to the skin. Great care must be exercised in selecting combs. The tips of the teeth must be rounded, otherwise vigorous combings can lacerate the skin. It is important, too, to select the proper coarseness or fineness of the comb. The thicker the coat the wider apart should be the teeth of the comb used. Wire rakes and brushes are often used to de-mat the coats of longhaired dogs but these need extreme care as they can easily tear the delicate underlying skin.

Grooming not only improves the general appearance of your dog, it also makes the animal feel better and helps to prevent the dog attracting parasites or developing skin diseases. Combined with proper exercise, consistent correct grooming helps to promote good muscle tone and general fitness. Grooming also helps to form a close bond between the dog and its owner – unless, of course, it is incorrectly carried out, or the wrong instruments are used, causing pain.

Some breeds, such as the terriers, need regular trimming to keep their coats in order. Unless you are able to carry out the trimming yourself, find a good canine beautician and make regular appointments to have your dog trimmed. Other breeds which may just need a little scissoring may be dealt with at home, and a little practice soon develops the necessary techniques.

Left: A Pembroke Corgi being groomed with a shortbristled brush to stimulate the skin and remove dead hair.

Right: A hound glove stimulates muscle tone and helps to impart a healthy glow to the coat of the shorthaired dog.

Grooming the longcoated dog

The small dog will need to stand on a convenient table or bench, while a taller dog can be groomed while it stands on the floor. You may have to sit on a low stool to get down to a comfortable level, and to avoid backache if the dog's coat needs a lot of work. It is important for a dog to learn to stand still for grooming, and if your dog is restless tie it up with a fairly short chain on its collar and talk soothingly.

Start at the rear end with one of the hindlegs. Lift the long outer hair with your free hand and use a suitable brush to work through all the undercoat down the thigh and lower leg. Use the brush gently down the inside of the thigh where the skin is particularly sensitive, then groom the longer top hairs back into place. Repeat this procedure with the other hindleg, then groom the hips and over the rump down the whole length of the tail. Check under the tail and remove any dry excreta, and tease out or clip any mats or badly soiled patches.

Next brush out the forelegs; again lift the longer top hairs, brush through the finer underhairs, then brush the top hairs back into place. The underbody comes next; this is very tender and sensitive in some dogs. If you acquire a dog which has not been properly looked after and is very matted underneath, have the hair professionally clipped away, then you can retrain the dog to accept grooming as the new hair grows. Brush right through the fine underbody hair, using short gentle strokes. Do not pull, and pay particular attention to the region between the thighs, along the belly and between the forelimbs. The hair here is fine and mats easily, and the skin is very tender. Grass seeds and twigs often get caught up in this fine hair and can cause discomfort. Unless your dog is going to be shown in competition, it is quite a good idea to trim away the hair in these areas, particularly if your dog takes a lot of exercise in woods or over farmland.

Groom the body hair over the shoulders, along the ribs and flanks to the hips, then brush along the spine. Groom down the chest and brush the ruff if present, then the long hair around the face and ears. After you have worked all over the dog with the brush, use a metal comb to deal with any feathering on the legs, tail and around the head. Use damp cotton or tissue to wipe inside the ear flaps.

Grooming the shortcoated dog

Follow the same general guidelines as for the longcoated dog, having selected a suitable brush or grooming glove for your dog's coat type. Start at the hind end, progress to the body and finish with the head. Any white areas can be rubbed with a chalk preparation to remove discoloration; the chalk preparation is then brushed out. Short fine coats benefit from applications of grooming powder to separate the hairs; short, close coats gleam after being buffed up with a silk scarf or a pad of warmed velvet.

Treating dry skin

Dry skin on the pads, the nose or around the eyes can be protected before exercise by an application of petroleum jelly, working this well into the skin and wiping away the surplus.

Right: The soft hair behind the ears is particularly prone to matting and must be carefully combed through, especially after exercise and in damp weather.

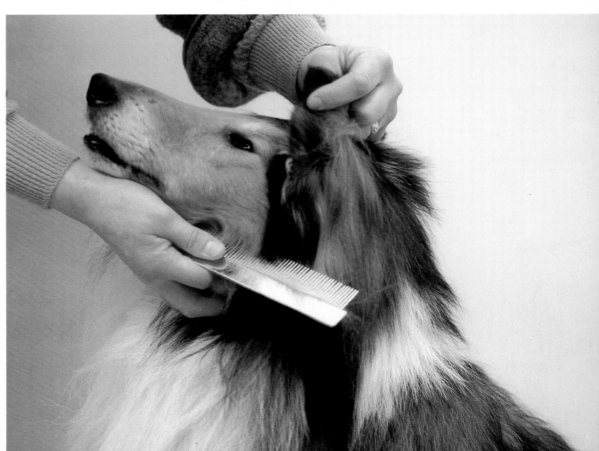

Left: Basic grooming care of the longcoated dog is designed to keep the coat free from mats and tangles.

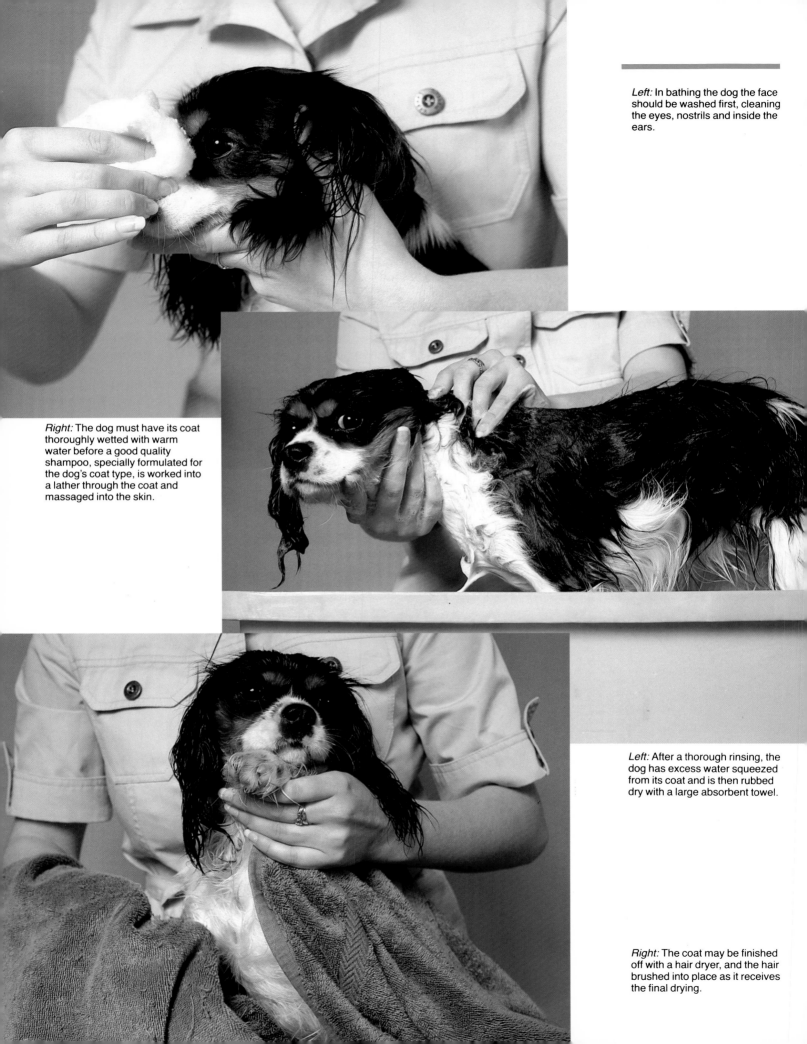

Left: In bathing the dog the face should be washed first, cleaning the eyes, nostrils and inside the ears.

Right: The dog must have its coat thoroughly wetted with warm water before a good quality shampoo, specially formulated for the dog's coat type, is worked into a lather through the coat and massaged into the skin.

Left: After a thorough rinsing, the dog has excess water squeezed from its coat and is then rubbed dry with a large absorbent towel.

Right: The coat may be finished off with a hair dryer, and the hair brushed into place as it receives the final drying.

Pet dogs which live indoors often shed lots of hair and may also smell, and therefore the dog needs to be bathed to make it socially acceptable. Some owners make regular appointments for their dogs to be professionally bathed, trimmed and groomed, but it is quite easy to bathe your own dog. Make sure your dog is given time to urinate before you begin. Small breeds can be bathed in a large bowl or sink, while larger breeds can either be washed in the family bath tub or stood in the yard near a drainage point, while warm water is poured over them from a bucket or spray. If your dog is bathed outdoors you should choose a warm day. If you use a sink or bathtub, place a small rubber mat or towel inside to help the dog feel safe and secure. Take great care to remove any mats or clumps of hair before you start. Once a mat is wetted, it is quite impossible to tease out, and it must then be removed by clipping it out at skin level.

A hand spray is ideal for wetting the coat through to the skin, and for giving the final rinsing. Alternatively you can use a jug or pan to ladle water over the dog. If your dog is lively, wear a plastic apron or even a light raincoat to protect your clothes from a soaking. Since bathing removes the natural oils which make a dog's coat weatherproof and warm, it should only be carried out when really necessary.

Take off your dog's collar and stand the animal in the bowl or tub. Carefully wash its face with a damp sponge and wipe out the ears. Smear vaseline along the eyelids, and put cotton wool into the ears to prevent water running down the ear canals. Thoroughly wet the coat from the neck down, then apply a shampoo suitable for your dog's coat type or condition. Follow the manufacturer's instructions, working up a good lather. Pay particular attention to between the toes and under the tail.

Use fresh warm water to rinse every trace of shampoo from the coat. Take care to keep the water out of the dog's eyes, nose and ears. The water should be comfortably warm, never hot or cold, and the temperature should be kept constant throughout the whole of the bathing process.

Once the dog has been thoroughly rinsed, squeeze the surplus water out of the coat, using both hands, working from the back down the limbs to the feet. Lift the dog out of the bath tub and wrap it in a large towel. Encourage the dog to give a good shake to get rid of more surplus water, then vigorously towel the coat. Change towels as they get wet and, if the dog finds it acceptable, use a hand-held hairdryer to dry the coat. If you do use a hairdryer, you can lift each section of the coat with a grooming brush, encouraging each section of the coat to lie in the desired direction. If you have a dog that requires regular bathing, it is worth investing in a special directional drier which does not need to be hand held.

Golden rules for bathing

Try to keep the dog at the same temperature throughout
Do not use too hot or too cold water
Keep water and shampoo out of the dog's eyes, ears and nose
Keep medicated shampoo away from the dog's genital area
Never bathe a dog with a matted coat
Rinse every trace of shampoo out of the coat
Do not delay the drying process
Position the coat as it dries
Keep the dog indoors until it is thoroughly dry

Index

PICTURE CREDITS

Animal Photography Limited/Sally Anne Thompson 18-19, 23, 37, 40, 46 bottom right, 48 bottom right, 49, 54 top, 55 bottom, 65 left, 68 bottom, 71 top, 73, 74-75, 84, 85, 107, 110, 111, 120, 126, 141 inset, 151, 156-157, 158, 159, 169 bottom, 176-177 **Ardea Photographics** 32, 36 top, 41 top right, 81 bottom, 95, 140, 169 top, 180-181 **Art Directors** 24-25, 144-145, 152-153 **Camerapix Hutchison** 10 top, 11 **Colorific!** 97, 178 **Robert Harding Associates** 14-15, 87 **Marc Henrie** 115 top, 179 **Michael Holford** 12, 13, 16 bottom, 17 **Eric and David Hosking** 90-91 **The Image Bank** 76-78, 81 top, 93 inset **Frank Lane** 9, 10 bottom, 105 **William MacQuitty** 143 **N.H.P.A.** 39, 42-43, 50 bottom, 53 right, 55 top, 57 right, 58, 62 right, 88, 168 **The Photosource** 38, 124, 174-175 **The Picture Library** 94-95 **Rex Features** 116 **Angela Sayer** 121 **Ronald Sheridan** 14 **Solitaire/Animal Graphics** 16 top, 33 top, 46 top, 46 bottom left, 47 right, 48 top, 51, 52, 53 left, 54 bottom, 56, 59 right, 60 bottom, 64, 66, 67, 68 top, 69, 70 bottom left, 71 bottom, 80, 82, 83, 92-93, 101 top, 102, 103, 106, 107 inset, 108, 109, 112-114, 115 bottom, 122, 125 top, 127-139, 141, 142, 148-150, 154, 157 inset, 161, 164-167, 170, 172-173, 182, 183 bottom left, 186, 188, 189 **Spectrum Colour Library** 20, 28-29, 31, 33 bottom, 35, 36 bottom, 41 bottom, 43 inset, 47 left, 48 bottom left, 62 left, 65 right, 70 top, 70 bottom right, 72 top, 89, 111 inset, 118-119, 123, 162-163, 183 bottom right, 184, 185, 187 **Zefa** title, contents, introduction, 8, 26-27, 34, 44-45, 50 top, 57 left, 59 left, 60 top, 61, 63, 72 bottom, 98, 99, 100, 101 bottom, 104, 117, 125 bottom